The Food Store

50+ Stunning Interior Designs & Branding Concepts

images
Publishing

Contents

Foreword

Text by Paolo Emilio Bellisario

Founding member of NINE associati, Emilio Bellisario is an architect and designer located in Italy and professor of the master's degree course in Interior Design of IED Milano. He was also the co-founder and CEO of ZO_ loft architecture and design—an award-winning collective of designers focusing on innovative, iconic, and flexible design products—as well as Editor and Head of External Relationships at *Cityvision* magazine. Emilio has contributed articles to several books and magazines and organized events, exhibitions, workshops, and international competitions, referring to the topics of globalization, urban utopias, and additive technologies. Winner of a number of important international prizes and awards, he has also been invited to exhibit—as architect and designer—in many international exhibitions. His work has been documented by the most important specialized magazines and publishings worldwide.

"You can't do the same thing in San Francisco [as] in Paris. What matters is the physical and conceptual context, which is why I need [to make] a very careful [analysis of the work], before designing: [by] studying history, literature, geography, even poetry and philosophy ... We have to invent a new solution [each time] and books help us."

This quote was by Gae Aulenti—one of the few well-known female architects working in Italy, distinguished by her innovative creations both in Italy and abroad, following a proactive vision linked to the past, but always strongly projected towards the future—and I strongly agree with her sentiments. While having a brand identity is definitely important, having a retail identity is becoming increasingly vital.

Having an identity—whatever it is—is the big deal. People want to identify themselves within a brand and that brand must have its own statement, a believing in which consumers can identify themselves. Similarly, the store must have its own identity that needs to coincide with that of the brand. The store space must express the same distinctiveness when customers are inside. As such, the brand identity needs to match with the shopping experience.

In an era in which Google, Pinterest, Instagram, Facebook, and other social media platforms have often replaced books and specialized magazines, the abuse of the internet and social networks, as project inspiration platforms, has levelled out. The online phenomenon has improved the designers' know-how, standardizing their concept, their mood-boards, their strategies, their design language, and their quality of projects, too. So retailers live within the paradox of being authentic and innovative and, at the same time, it is much more challenging to emerge and stand out from competitors.

What to do then?

The first point is using the shop as a medium to tell and involve in a learning path while shopping. The second point is enabling connections with the territory. On the one hand, then, retail designers must be able to interpret a project brief, analyzing brand's competitors, understanding the brand's values, and sensing the market changes focusing on the most flexible, exportable, and repeatable solution, too.

On the other hand—as Gae Aulenti always stressed during her life and as I, too, believe—going back to the physical context, the history, the local materials, looking at local craftsmanship and typical workmanship, or simply analyzing the society, the people's needs, their habits, it becomes a fundamental starting point for designers who are asked to create a retail project.

Being able to interpret or re-interpret both of these elements allows retail designers to develop a unique creative strategy, their personal expressive language to describe the brand experience to customers in an innovative way. This is a design attitude

that becomes even more important when retail designers are working with a start-up company, or an historic brand renewing itself, because with their design project, they will actively collaborate in the writing of a new story.

In 2009, Simon Sinek said during a famous TED Talk, "People don't buy what you do; they buy why you do it." His quote is still relevant today when consumers are becoming more interested in backstories rather than simply in what they're buying.

Most businesses have a description of what they do; however, not many have yet had a deeper discussion of why they do it, but what works now is finding the people that believe in what you believe. You could provide customers with the best product and all the information about it, but if the customer doesn't trust the brand, it's worthless. When creating the retail experience and before selling the customer on the product, the designer should focus on selling the brand statement, providing the customer with a reason—a why—to spend their time and money.

For instance, many go to Starbucks for the experience. The great value that these chains convey is based on the idea that the customer's experience at the point of sale must be special and unique. The customer must feel at ease in the environment and, above all, must live and recognize the same experience by entering every sales point in the chain.

But how can this sense of recognition be created?

The customers in the store undergo an emotional experience, relying on nostalgia, originality, talent, surprise, and so forth. The consumers must identify themselves with the brand and give it a symbolic value thanks to the sensations, the images, and the perceptions that the brand is able to arouse. So, the answer is the personalization and the uniqueness of the customer experience in the stores.

Brands know that when entering the store consumers are looking for something memorable that they can then share on social media. Consumers are looking for Seth Godin's "Purple Cow" (*Purple Cow: Transform Your Business by Being Remarkable,* 2003). In today's society, consumers now have everything they want, they just have to choose, but they don't have the time and, above all, the desire to listen to the advertisements that are offered to them.

Providing a sufficiently extraordinary experience can attract innovators who, with their enthusiasm, can spread the idea. A "Purple Cow" is the extraordinary—for which it is worth talking about—that will make itself a positive marketing experience, and will expand like a virus, first within the otaku (computer nerds) and then gradually towards all other consumers.

A "Purple Cow" is not a shortcut, but it is the best and perhaps the only way to achieve a result. There is no way of

knowing whether it will be successful or not. In a crowded market the best choice is to try to emerge; to follow the others means to fail.

So the new task for the retail designer is to turn the brand and its statement into a remarkable three-dimensional environment in which consumers may walk into, interact, and entertain themselves with the brand. This is an innovative human-centered and multidisciplinary approach: it's not just about designing a space, but also what it offers to users.

Retail designers must be able to manage both technical strategic sides of a project, starting from an accurate analysis, and to provide the best solutions in terms of space enhancement and service design. They are being asked to create spaces that convey strong feelings, combined with the right selection of furniture, lights, materials, and colors. If this has been done correctly, the retail experience will be remarkable, the customer will become loyal, and they will tell someone about the brand.

Case Studies

Gaudenti 1971—Vittorio Emanuele II

lamatilde

Turin, Italy

3165 square feet
(294 square meters)

2017

Combining both a small Italian fine pastry shop with a large international bakery, the design brief for Gaudenti 1971 was to create a space that could convey respect for the traditional values and culture of Italian confectionery with a strong drive for renewal.

Systematically integrating new décor features, the project involved the careful renovation of the existing elements. While a different graphic motif was designed for each venue, giving a new interpretation of the historical decorative styles, the consistent use of velvet and blue ensured the brand was instantly recognizable.

Inside one of Turin's oldest fine pastry shops, all of the elements with historical value were recovered and enhanced, while those that hindered an optimal use of space were redirected to a new use—such as the windows, which were turned into little sitting areas. All additions were custom designed: the counter, for example, contrasted against the classic wood paneling with its spaceship-like quality.

The two-tier tables were designed especially for Gaudenti 1971 with a handy touch of innovation; halfway between a coffee table and a lounge table, they were both functional spaces for customers and an exposure point for the products on display—all handcrafted in a vast and fully equipped prep room on the floor below.

The design of Gaudenti 1971 displayed a harmonious union between the historical décor and a sympathetic contemporary update, creating a space that was both traditional and fresh and able to dialogue with its own heritage in a surprising and brilliant way.

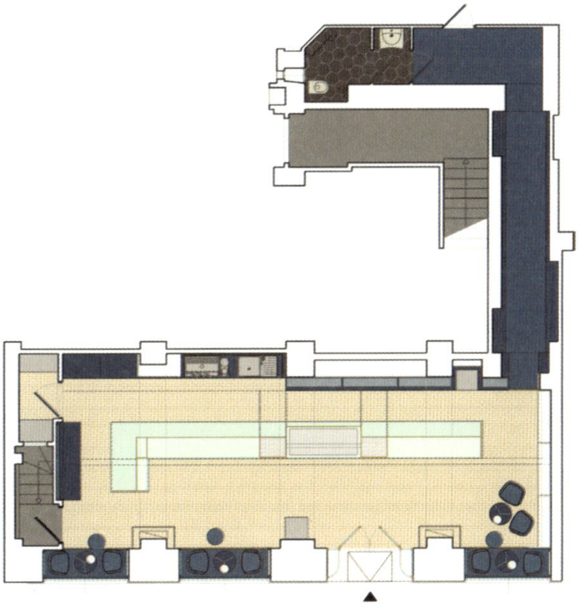

Belle Époque

Mind Design

London, United Kingdom

646 square feet (60 square meters)

2014

Belle Époque is a boutique French pâtisserie on Upper Street in London specializing in high-end pastry creations.

The identity of the brand was based on the drawings by English Art Nouveau artist Aubrey Beardsley. As such, the logo was designed to be relatively simple as the emphasis was on the pattern and photography. Additionally, the typography linked the Art Nouveau period with the hippie movement of the 1960s.

Besides the overall print, web design, packaging, signage, and some interior design, Mind Design also developed a photo concept that linked the products with the overall identity.

The original black façade of the shop was kept and the projection sign makes a reference to the curved frame of the windows. The window display of small cakes attracts passers-by. The interior is in lighter colors and features a large marble

counter. The display space on the back shows mostly bread products as well as chocolates and snacks.

Special attention was given to the curved golden lamps over the counter, which link the interior to the identity design. The overall feel is a transparent and light interpretation of a traditional local shop.

BELLE ÉPOQUE
PATISSERIE

PATISSERIE
Free
belleepoque.co.uk
Loyalty
Card

Islington
belleepoque.co.uk
BELLE ÉPOQUE
PATISSERIE
PATISSERIE
Newington Green
call +44 (0)20 7249 2222
come to Nº37 Newington Green, London N16 9PR
from Monday to Wednesday 8am to 6pm,
Thursday to Friday 8am to 7pm,
Saturday 9am to 7pm, Sunday 9am to 6pm
visit belleepoque.co.uk

BELLE ÉPOQUE

Coconut Pastelería

Nihil Estudio

Torrent, Spain

2045 square feet
(190 square meters)

2017

Just as the best confectionery requires quality ingredients and care in the preparation of each cake, the design of Coconut Pastelería by Nihil Estudio was treated in the same way.

The idea of a portion of a cake lead to the interior design. Nihil Studio extended this throughout the entire process, passing through the open areas to the public and giving the work areas a meticulous aesthetic. With a materiality that fragments the space horizontally, three layers of materials, textures, and different chromatic ranges were generated as a nod to the ingredients of a cake. With a painted-tile base, the tiled walls and ceiling were reminiscent of the part that embellishes and culminates the sweets. This element also crossed and connected, at the same time, the area of the shop and the zone of purchase and consumption of coconut.

Coconut Pastelería was born from the respect to the technique and the artisan quality of the pastry work. Following this

theme that speaks of tradition and the avant-garde, the interior was made more spacious, comfortable, and aesthetic. A new workshop can be opened to the public via glass, showing transparency in the production, while allowing the entry of natural light into the work area. Even from the street, people can appreciate the craft work through the open space, which also allows privacy for the workers. Simultaneously, baskets were hung in the shop's window to recall tradition while also serving as a support to the counter.

This link between the traditional and the avant-garde extended from the pastry to the graphic design. Different design techniques employed by Nihil Estudio maintained the essence of the premises while combining fonts and colors that, like the interior design of the bakery, generated a harmonic flow. The material and chromatic combination used in the interior design followed the graphic design, which was also used for the labels, cards, and even the clothes of the workers, and a packaging that goes from the boxes for the cakes to the coffee glasses.

COCO
PASTELERÍA

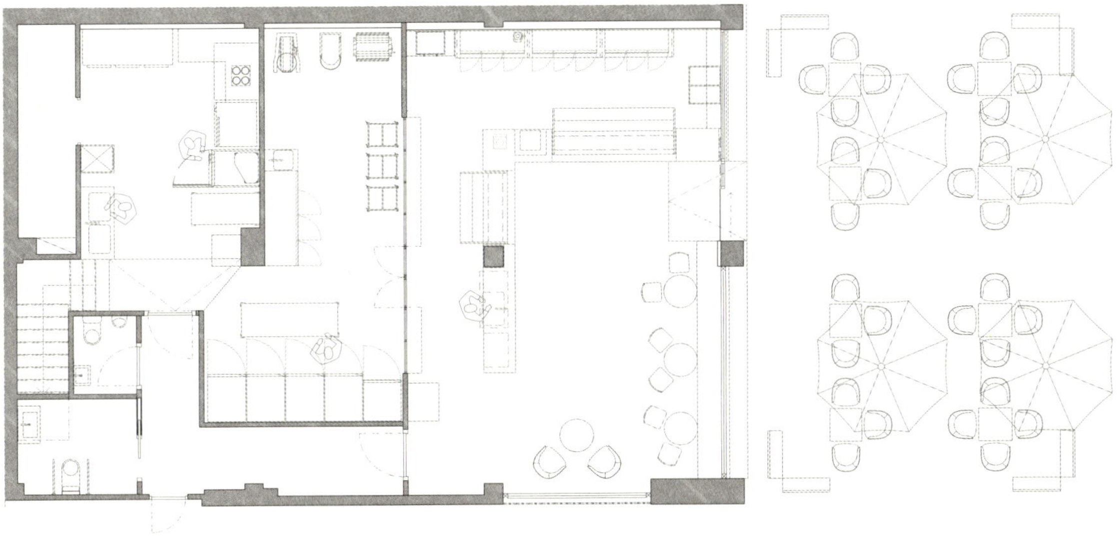

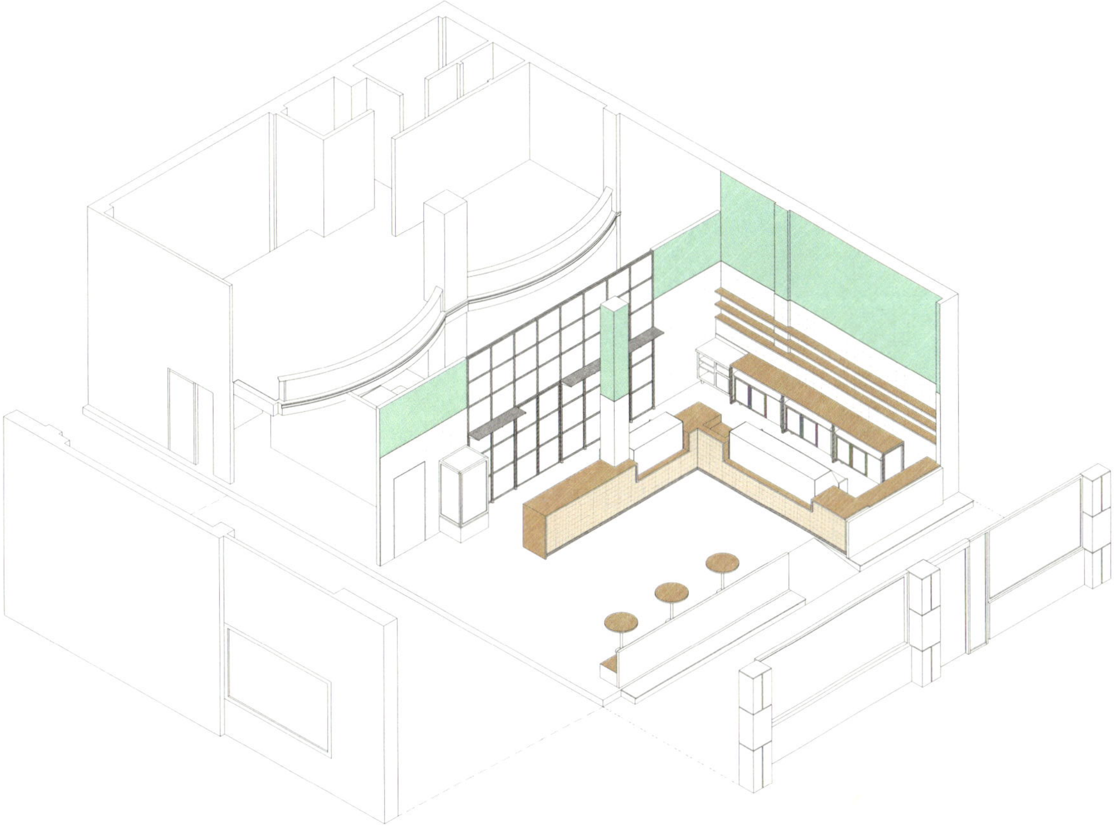

Flour and Salt Bakery

Pentagram

Taipei, China

1668 square feet
(155 square meters)

2017

Flour and Salt Bakery is a chain of stores based in Taipei offering local and international baked goods and specialty food and drinks prepared with a focus on organic ingredients.

Pentagram was appointed to design the branding for the market-style restaurant, which involved creating a name from its ingredients—"flour" and "salt"—to become an iconic identity. Additionally, the project tackled the design of the interiors, the graphics, and creation of environmental packaging.

The name of the chain was derived from the purity and authenticity of the baked goods and their ingredients. It works well in both Chinese and English, and in the Chinese version, there is a double meaning in one of the characters, which also stands for "conversation." The English typography was set in Sofia Pro Black and Chinese characters were custom designed.

The straightforward construction of the name was complemented by a logo comprised of simple graphic icons

represented by custom shapes that suggest a flour particle and a salt crystal. The two elements were connected by a looping symbol meaning "and," influenced by Japanese handwriting, which is commonly used throughout Asia.

The color palette chosen was a utilitarian black and white, which was also used on the packaging. The contemporary look and feel stands out from other restaurants in the marketplace, which often employ an illustrative approach and earth tones to appear organic.

The identity was integrated into the restaurant interiors, also designed by Pentagram. The shapes of the logo repeat in the custom-designed tiles in the floor and the neon pendant lamps in the ceiling. The branding was echoed in environmental graphics that activate the space with patterns. The designers created a system of food and drink pictograms, which were integrated into the custom black-and-white wallpaper and etched into the wooden panels. Signage was understated, with the logo on an exterior façade and a functional magnetic menu board at the main counter.

As part of the interior design, the team developed the layout of the restaurant. The interior of Flour and Salt was crafted to be a large and open market-style space loosely

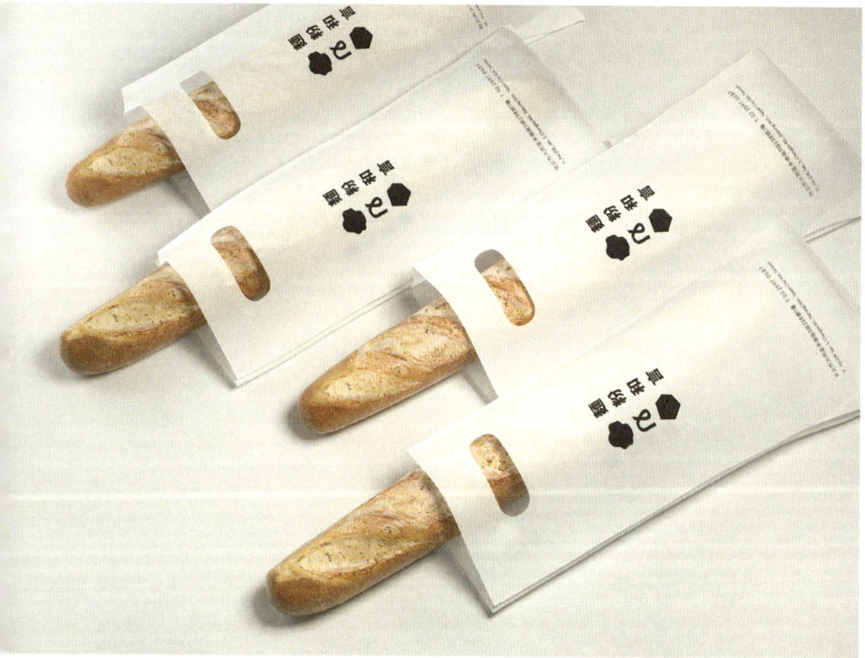

divided into different sections, with retail and product displays mixed in with dining areas. Modular shelving units were constructed of plywood pegboards that could be easily moved around and repositioned, providing versatility in the display layout.

The front-of-house service area was subdivided into five stations. The circulation of the service counter functions in a linear manner, with the point-of-sale at the far end. The two types of seating include a quick bar-level table aligned with the glass windows of the façade and was subdivided between a communal bar table and bar seating in pairs. In the rear, sit-down banquette seating was created for guests looking to dine at a more leisurely pace.

Home Bakery

Blacksheep

Dubai, UAE

990 square feet
(92 square meters)

2014

Home Bakery was born out of a natural love of baking and a passion for how the simple act of eating dessert makes people feel so happy.

What originated as a business in a home kitchen soon expanded with overflowing orders from a loyal established customer base and a barrage of new enquiries in the form of fanatic social media followers, both equally inspired by the creativity, beauty, and taste of the desserts produced. As demand began to greatly outweigh supply, it was time to turn the Home Bakery business into a brand.

Blacksheep were approached to create a brand identity translated across a range of packaging and collateral, and the interior design of the first store in Dubai. Although the business was soon to become a commercial operation, it was fundamental that it retained as much of the passion and personality of the desserts themselves. The brand needed to reflect the simplicity and authenticity of the home business while

the store needed to act as a home away from home for customers, old and new.

Blacksheep created a brand DNA based on the core value "simple indulgence." From this, a visual identity was created, using three different design elements all derived from the emotionally evocative and sensory pleasure experienced when we eat sweet foods. The elements consisted of a wordmark, brandmark, and a bespoke gradient.

The Home Bakery wordmark was created using a unique set of hand-drawn letterforms—these letterforms referenced classic typefaces used for literary design, and a sense of handcrafting was communicated through the wordmarks irregular qualities. The wordmark represented the simple origins of the brand and also emphasized how the desserts themselves were made: by hand. Six brandmark variations were then created to reference baking in the most literal sense—the sprinkling of cocoa or icing sugar—and the shape of Home Bakery's most popular product: the Chewy Melt cookie.

Two colors were merged to create a vertical gradient to represent the physical high experienced when sweet food is eaten. These colors were taken from the classic ingredient of Arabic baking—the pistachio nut. Starting with a

deep green and steadily growing to a peach, the gradient speaks of the neutrality of the customer before they taste sweetness and the euphoria they experience after.

The store interior needed to reflect the origins and values of the brand. Blacksheep were conscious that the store should feel as much like a home as possible—the bakery's home. They developed a house-like structure within the internal framework of the restaurant, creating an atmosphere of homeliness, warmth, and comfort.

The house structure was made visible from both entry points and also acts as a functional design element by curving inwards to create bench seating.

Windows and translucent frames give customers views into the kitchen, allowing them to enjoy the theatre of the baking taking place. Earthy materials and furnishings such as rustic oak timber, thick padded fabric, and worn leather allow the simple deliciousness of the products to speak for themselves.

Home Bakery
LITTLE BITES
MACAROONS
BROWNIES
CRONUTS

Supreme

Lust auf Vollkorn—concept store

TOC. designstudio

Weissenstadt, Germany

2153 square feet
(200 square meters)

2015

In trend with the modern drive for people to enjoy more natural and authentic foods with a healthier focus, the design of the Lust auf Vollkorn concept store sought to communicate this along with the philosophy of the brands Pema and Leupoldt. The design was characterized by a contemporary interpretation of traditional values, as both companies enjoyed a long history of more than 100 years. Pema is a specialist bakery for wholegrain bread, while Leupoldt manufactures traditional gingerbread.

The design of the concept store infused an interpretation of the company values—including the tradition, high quality of the ingredients, simplicity of the recipes, as well as authenticity—into a modernized setting. The design was a combination of natural, tactile materials and smooth, modern structures with fine graphics. Warm colors like dark brown and gold gave a noble background and contrast with accents in strong violet. All in all, the design offered a perfect stage for the whole grain combined with a fresh kick.

The tables were positioned as both product displays and dining areas, allowing customers to eat the goods and study the products on the shelf at the same time—and if they liked the taste, they could purchase products to take home easily. Creative tastings also helped to awaken the taste for whole grain in customers, while showcasing the tradition and innovation of the products.

GENUSS
Herzlich Willkommen in der Welt von »Lust auf Vollkorn«
8
10

NATÜRLICH ROGGEN-VOLLKORNBROT
NATURALLY WHOLE GRAIN RYE BREAD

BIS BALD
FÜR DICH
GUTEN APPETIT
VON HERZEN
DANKE SCHÖN
DANKE SCHÖN
BIS BALD
FÜR DICH

Leupoldt
MANUFAKTUR SEIT 1905

NATÜRLICH REIN

Lust auf Vollkorn

M Tang

Out of Thin Air Studio

Ningbo, China

861 square feet (80 square meters)

2017

Inspired by the elegant desserts and colorful candies produced by the client, the design team aspired to create a perfect dessert space for customers to enjoy these sweet offerings in Ningbo, China.

After investigating the site and analyzing the surrounding environment, the design team decided to create a graceful interior space to highlight the style of the desserts. Moreover, some special facilities were provided for the main target groups, such as booths designed specifically for children, tables for friends to have afternoon tea, and bar areas for singles. The overall style sought to be "simple, elegant, and refreshing."

Rendering was done with bright yellow paint so that M Tang could be recognized by foodies from a distance. As the square footage was limited, folding windows were installed at the bar areas—when windows were fully open, interconnection between interior and exterior spaces could be achieved while enlarging the shop visually. As such, the atmosphere inside and outside the shop were united.

Between the two columns in the space, the design team positioned four flexible tables. The columns—fitted with spotlights—were enclosed with high-transparency tempered glass, which could be used to post brand information and activity notices to promote the brand.

Cement floor paint was used largely on the ground; honeycomb bricks were paved subtly around the central column. The design of the bar area at the entrance was characterized by a minimalist style.

The stone, walls, wooden doors, and the instruments were all made to be white and the bar was made of natural marble of the same color scheme.

The refined interior and French flavor succeeded in adding to the experience of enjoying the delicate desserts.

M
tang
英式下午茶 | 甜品

胖哥俩

M TANG

Laura's Bakery—Værnedamsvej

Johannes Torpe Studios

Copenhagen, Denmark

807 square feet
(75 square meters)

2015

Tucked away in a courtyard on the cozy street of Værnedamsvej in Copenhagen, this cozy boutique-style bakery was the latest addition to the Laura's Bakery family. The small and narrow space took full advantage of the modular design concept and even left room for two small areas for indoor seating.

Part of a chain of gourmet bakeries, the design drew on the nostalgia of grandmother-style cakes and bread, integrated with the combination of a modern metropolitan vibe and a minimalistic Scandinavian aesthetic.

Together with the client, Johannes Torpe Studios built the brand from scratch handling concept creation, visual identity, and interior design. Since the opening of the first shop, the concept expanded across multiple locations, additionally introducing a pizza concept to selected stores, as well as a street-food concept with food trucks and ice-cream bicycles.

In many bakeries, the cakes are put on display while the bread lives a silent life on the back wall. In this project, they wanted to bring the bread forward, making it the focus of the space and, thus, the foundation for the design. Laura's Bakery produces high-quality bread and cakes using classic techniques and the best ingredients. To communicate the nature of the products, they chose a foundation of bare materials such as solid wood, concrete, steel, and subway tiles. Together, the modest and industrial materials create a raw aesthetic that emphasizes the raw and natural qualities of the bread.

The visual identity of Laura's Bakery was completely conceptualized across all elements of the brand, including interiors, graphics, and packaging, which merged together to create one holistic experience of the brand. The earthy tones on the cover of the outside of the packaging were complemented by a selection of contrasting colors on the inside.

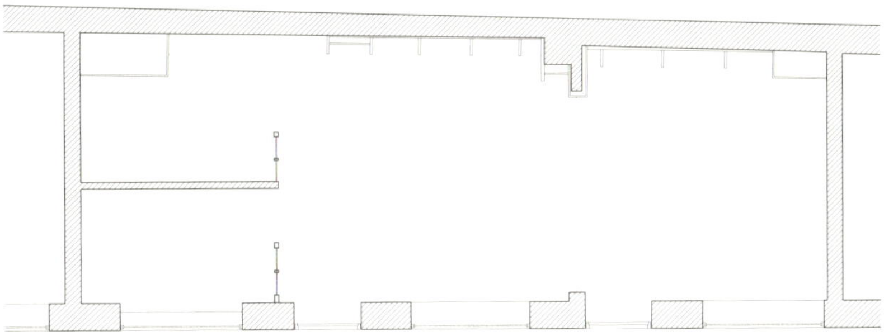

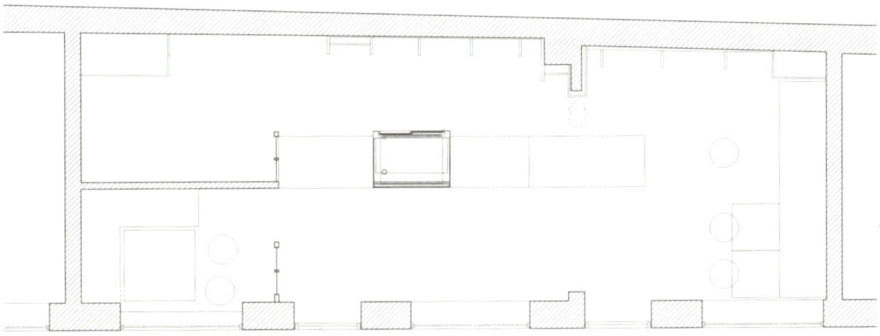

Ciambelleria Alonzi

NINE associati

Sora, Italy

269 square feet
(25 square meters)

2015

Handing down the craft secret of food and confectionary traditions since 1890—including the secret processing the ciambella sorana bread—the historic Italian Ciambelleria Alonzi required a new look and enlisted NINE associati to help them achieve it.

Situated in the center of Sora—hometown of Cardinal Cesare Baronio—the family-run artisan company of over six generations used limited machinery, preferring manual techniques, to enhance the organoleptic qualities of the products cooked in its oven.

Driven by the need to renew the old wood-oven and baking spaces that were no longer adequate for the fast-paced retail shop that complemented the bakery, NINE associati worked with the limited area—269 square feet (25 square meters)—to transform the old workspace into more an optimal and flexible floorplan. The new shop was designed to be able to adapt to both baking and sales and allow for reconfiguration if

required over time, without adjusting the masonry or having to change the furniture.

The concept of their trademark Sallecone biscuit (made with legume and carob flours) was inspired by one of the city's little-known historic figures, Cardinal Cesare Baronio. The biscuit worked as both a delightful product for visitors to take away and a useful device for sharing a unique aspect of the city's cultural identity.

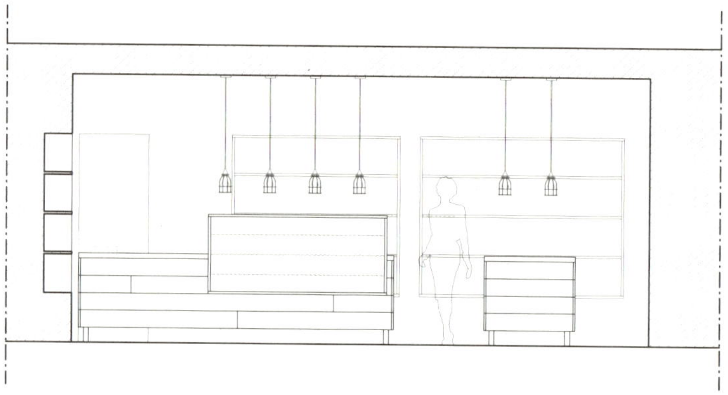

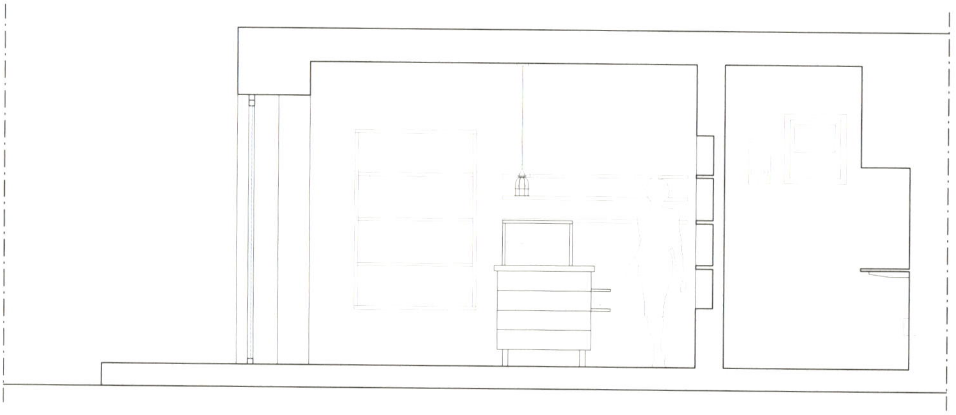

CATOLE
PER
ONFEZIONI
REGALO

Daniel Bakery

moodley brand identity (Sabine Kernbichler), Florian Weitzer

Vienna, Austria

3875 square feet (360 square meters)

2015

Located at Hotel Daniel in Vienna, Austria, moodley brand identity was engaged to design not only the hotel space, but also the interior and branding for Daniel Bakery.

The bakery, situated on the ground floor of this popular hotel, had become a popular culinary hot spot in Vienna specializing in sweet specialties, such as cheesecake, pavlova, ginger shortbread, cookies, and cupcakes.

Whether enjoying a drink or a homemade pastry, having a business meeting or chilling out with friends, the space attracted many patrons.

Honing its focus on only what modern consumers really needed, without any unnecessary detail, moodley brand identity created a clever and luxurious space that was confident and unpretentious; subtle, but with a slight personal touch and small playful elements.

The relaxed interior couples the organic tones and textures of timber and plenty of indoor plants with luminous natural light, while a long serving counter in white and woodgrain punctuates the space while providing plenty of access points for attending to customers from early in the morning until late at night.

HEY HONEY
DANIEL
HEY HONEY
DANIEL

WÄREN
ALOIS DANIEL
DANIEL

So schmeckt
die Steiermark...
Fresh Ideas.

Mökki

Blacksheep

Astana, The Republic of Kazakhstan

5382 square feet (500 square meters)

2017

With an ever-increasing population in the city, The Ritz-Carlton Astana saw an opportunity to engage a new market by creating a sophisticated, aspirational space where none had previously existed. The integration of food and drinks was a natural step for The Ritz-Carlton.

Blacksheep created a unique food experience to firmly resonate with the new audience of a young capital, set to spearhead creativity and progress in Kazakhstan. Aiming to design an offer intrinsically connected to Astana, Blacksheep wove together the old and new with tradition and innovation harmoniously.

The design team established the strategy, naming, and food direction for the offer within the Talan Towers complex, with the distinctive persona driving the design of the space and its overall identity.

Mökki, meaning "to be a home," sits on the third floor and was designed to deliver an engaging experience for guests from morning to night. Three design pillars were

developed—honesty, simplicity, and craftsmanship—and these informed all decisions. Delivering a complete guest experience meant that each touch point of Mökki was carefully considered and curated, from the brand and wider interior design to details such as the bespoke display holders and staff uniforms.

The space was designed to encourage exploration, with a variety of different areas, while the application of the brand throughout was uncontrived, respecting the design pillars established. This allowed the food to be the hero, celebrating craft, while respecting both seasonality and locality.

MÖKKI
MÖKKI

BAKERY

Chocolate chip

Danish
Fruit danish

MÖKKi

Meet Mia

Marita Bonačić, Negra Nigoević

Zagreb, Croatia

861 square feet
(80 square meters)

2015

A Croatian cake shop located in Zagreb, designers Marita Bonačić and Negra Nigoević were approached to create the name, visuals and packaging, product design, interior, styling, and photo shooting of the store, which needed to be unified to write the branding story.

Based on the catchphrase and name of the store—"Meet Mia"—the architects decided to approach the interior design from a meeting-place perspective, which lead to the space's first signature element: a large luminous "HEY" welcoming sign. This lighting piece also dictated other lighting elements in the interior, with frosted white LED bulbs evenly dispersed across the ceiling over the two zones becoming the leitmotif. Soft ambient lighting (apart from the "HEY" sign), pendants, and an oversized felt "hat" chandelier was situated in one zone, with a copper "candlestick" in the other.

Wedding gray walls, oak flooring, and white ceramic tile, hexagonal ceramic tile was used to spill into the timber floors and

even travel up the walls to create depth and character. The furniture—including padded benches, fixed circular tables, and upholstered seats—have the typology of a 1950s diner.

Copper was used as an accent color and to offer texture to the plush setting. Mainly found in the décor, it was also placed in the chandelier and seating, as well as plumbing tubes used to hang vertical gardens, menus and daily offerings.

6
7

HEY
MIAS SPECIALS

TAKE ME OUT

TOILETTE

Mister Baker

STIRIXIS Group

Dubai, United Arab Emirates

1076 square feet (100 square meters)

2017

Award: International Property Awards Dubai

Founded in 1990 with a network of 18 stores across the UAE, Mister Baker is the UAE's leading bakery chain. Based on newly agreed strategic guidelines, STIRIXIS Group was enlisted to redesign the logo and branding.

The logo of the brand had been kept the same since 1990—a personified sweet chef who indicated by the gesture of his fingers that the products sold where excellent. Although recognizable and well established in the minds of customers, it was decided it would be updated while maintaining all of the existing values of the brand promoted through the logo itself.

The characteristic gesture of the chef with his "okay" hand and the blink of his eye were again used in the new approach. The result was a modern logo, where the values, the image, and the information characterizing the brand were transmitted through the design.

Pomegranate and light blue were the two colors introduced to the brand in the new

approach. These vibrant colors were selected for the emotions the brand wanted to create for its customers. The feelings of happiness, joy, but also long-standing reassurance were transferred to the brand's new identity.

Moreover, STIRIXIS Group designed a new architectural and operational concept and organized the roll-out throughout the chain. The store's layout changed radically to comply with the new concept. The back counters were eliminated and the fridges were pushed to the walls, and island displays were used to promote certain products. Through these changes, the store opened up, bringing staff and customers closer together. Additionally, the

coffee area was upgraded with inspiring vivid colors, cake scents, and soothing music. Simultaneously, Mister Baker successfully designed and introduced new and amazing cakes and savory bites in complete alignment with the updated strategy and worked further in optimizing customer service in the new stores. The new holistic concept offers a whole new in-store experience driving its customers to truly celebrate every possible occasion and make every moment count.

The concept has already been implemented in the five biggest selling stores of the network with impressive results and was awarded at the International Property Awards Dubai 2018–2019.

Success
Surprises
Let's Celebrate
Traditions
Love

Gard'Ann Patisserie

kissmiklos

Kaposvár, Hungary

646 square feet
(60 square meters)

2017

Located in the centre of Kaposvár, a country town in Hungary, Gard'Ann Patisserie is well-known to the locals, as in 1928 the local shop of the Stühmer Chocolate Factory started its operations there. The interior equipment and furnishings of Stühmer Café were remarkable and kept under heritage protection. As such, when kissmiklos started the project, it sought to change the interior while protecting the heritage listing.

The name Gard'Ann was created through a merging of the word "garden" and the owner's name, Anne Marie, achieving a French-like sound that well-befitted the famous French confectionery. This was carried into the logo, which offered a bold typographic aesthetic.

The interior was designed as a contemporary interpretation of the classic grand cafés of the early 20th century. With the original counter painted in pastel green, the designer chose to expand this palette and paint the whole space in this shade, apart from the service corridor, which became pastel pink.

From a design perspective, pastel colors in pâtisseries are evocative of macaroons and other French cakes in the consumers' mind, so kissmiklos tried to create a balance between green, golden tones, and pastels in the space.

Among the pastel green, deeper shades of green were sought. As such, kissmiklos composed a huge picture on the main wall—a pattern from many old illustrations, leaves, plants, and birds (compiled from several different bird species). These illustrations were used throughout the whole visual identity: boxes, cards, paper bags, and so forth, thus strengthening the relationship with the garden theme.

The result was an elegant interior with a lovely little "French Bohemian" twist. The very bright interior full of greens, palms, and pastels conspires to make guests feel more relaxed.

GARD'ANN
CUKRÁSZDA

Welcome to the
GARDEN of FLAVORS

GARD'ANN
BOLDOG

Pâtisserie NUMOROUS

KOM Design Labo inc. (Jun Takagi +Moe Ishibashi)

Matsumoto-city, Japan

495 square feet (46 square meters)

2016

Combining novelty, humor, and authenticity to create the ambience of a laboratory, this pâtisserie located in Matsumoto-city enlisted KOM Design Labo to craft their branding and design to achieve an exciting space that would be different from the usual cake shop.

The name of the shop, Numorous, was a cheeky slant on the word "humorous," as such, the owners sought to inject this whimsy into the design. By applying a red slanting line to the word "humorous," which in Japanese is "Okashi-na-sama" (which also sounds like "cake-like" as "Okashi," also means "cake"), it made the perfect design for the pâtisserie.

To reflect the cake shop and saké (rice wine), for the logo the designers reinvented the original concept in a playful way by using a test tube and a round bottom flask reminiscent of a laboratory, which, when looked at in a certain way, form the single kanji (saké).

Immediately upon opening, the shop was flooded with interviews from newspapers, television, and magazines. After only a year, it became a leading pâtisserie in the city of Matsumoto.

NUMOROUS

NUMOROUS

Tafelzier Patisserie

TOC. designstudio

Nuremberg, Germany

1184 square feet
(110 square meters)

2017

Tafelzier Patisserie first opened its doors in 2017 when owner and pâtissier Jens Brockerhof—who had always been fascinated by the perfection and sensuality of French pastry making—decided to inspire the people of Nuremberg with "sweet works of art."

In intensive workshops with the pastry chef, the team of TOC. designstudio developed a unique concept around the world of the pâtisserie. From naming and interior design to corporate design, photos, packaging design, and corporate wording, everything came from the hands of the interdisciplinary office.

The concept that TOC. designstudio developed for the brand included the idea of expressing the change of seasons, not only in the product, but also in the interior design and corporate design. The change was treated similarly to the fashion industry, which changes the collection twice a year.

The overall appearance of the brand was minimalist and elegant—a style with soft,

subtle tones. White and gray with copper details met the current colors of the season. For spring and summer, these became orange and red tones, and dark green tones in winter.

In addition to the large refrigerated counter for fresh pâtisserie products, the packaged goods were presented on an oversized cake, atop of which a white gorilla winks. A tasting area in the store allows customers to enjoy the sweet delicacies along with a coffee in soft lounge armchairs.

In order to meet the high precision of the pâtissier's craftsmanship, the counter and built-in components

TAFELZIER
Patisserie

were planned and implemented as individual custom-made products. Thus, for example, the cladding of the refrigerated display counter with the different temperature ranges was designed as a jointless cube.

The lighting system used special luminaires, the light color of which enabled optimal presentation of the sweets. Floor-to-ceiling light walls were positioned in the shop windows, allowing the products to shine outwards. The theme of the light walls also changed with the seasonal change of the products.

The branding was used to develop a storytelling concept that was implemented in advertisements, billboards, packaging, and interior design.

Premier Cru
100% Arabica
le mystère d'Élise
ESPRESSO
ROSÉ BRUT
/ 59,00 €
ESPRESSO
D'ÉLISE
100% Arabica
33% Brasilien, 33% Indien, 33% Peru
mittelkräftig, schokoladig, nussig
Unsere exklusive Weihnachtsröstung, die besonders gut zu unseren süss-sündigen Produkten aus der Winterkollektion d'Élise passt
/ 10,50 €

le mystère d'Élise
le mystère d'Élise

le mystère d'Élise
ESPRESSO
le mystère d'Élise

TAFELZIER
Patisserie

PavoMea

Jansword Design, TGSP

Beijing, China

6458 square feet
(600 square meters)

2017

Awards: Nest Award
(Gold Award)

PavoMea is an artsy dessert brand that focuses on creating new desserts and snacks combining artistic elements. The designers picked up the great German chromatist Goethe as the brand soul, as it is he who discovered the residue and developed the hexagon color chrome.

Goethe thought the meanings of the color rely on the feelings of human beings, not the scientific statistic, as Newton thought. This coincides with what the brand wanted to convey—to enjoy yourself with sweets in colors of feelings. The brand logo refered to the image of Goethe, which comes from his famous painting portrait *Goethe in the Roman Campagna* in Frankfurt. It was transferred into a modern linear semi-abstract form located within a hexagon frame. The nose on the face was replaced by a prism-like triangle, indicating the relationship between colors and the light.

The logo can transfer into three modes to emphasize the concept of prism and show more contrast of lines and shapes. The

design dissolves into a pure white color scheme to present its panchromatic feature. Hologram paper was used to convey the brand tone. The prism shape was used as the macaroon package and hexagon shape for the small cake package. Six animals from Goethe's poem 'Lily's Menagerie' were picked as the accessory shapes.

Located at the 798 art zone in Beijing, hexagons, triangles, white tones, and accessory shapes were applied to the interior designs as an echo of the brand identity.

PAVOMEA
ARTSY DESSERT 本宮

Pâtisserie Es-T

KOM Design Labo inc. (Jun Takagi+Ikumi Miyazaki)

Nagoya-city, Japan

1528 square feet (142 square meters)

2015

Located in Nagoya-city, Japan, Pâtisserie Es-T offers unique and inspired products baked by the owner, who aspired for a playfulness to be incorporated in the interior design of the shop to match the goods on offer. Thus, Masato Shiba enlisted KOM Design Labo to achieve it.

A key element in the branding of the pâtisserie was to express the manual skills and meticulous labor of its pâtissier—a specialist in cakes, chocolate, and bread—that set it apart from other bakeries in the marketplace.

The logo design was based on two prominent colors that represent the two brand lines—"family" and "women."

Cuisine
Especially line
Treasure line
Cafe space
pâtisserie
Es-T

pâtisserie Es-T

pâtisserie
Es-T

Cuisine
Especially line
Treasure line
Cafe space

Special Gift
for
YOU

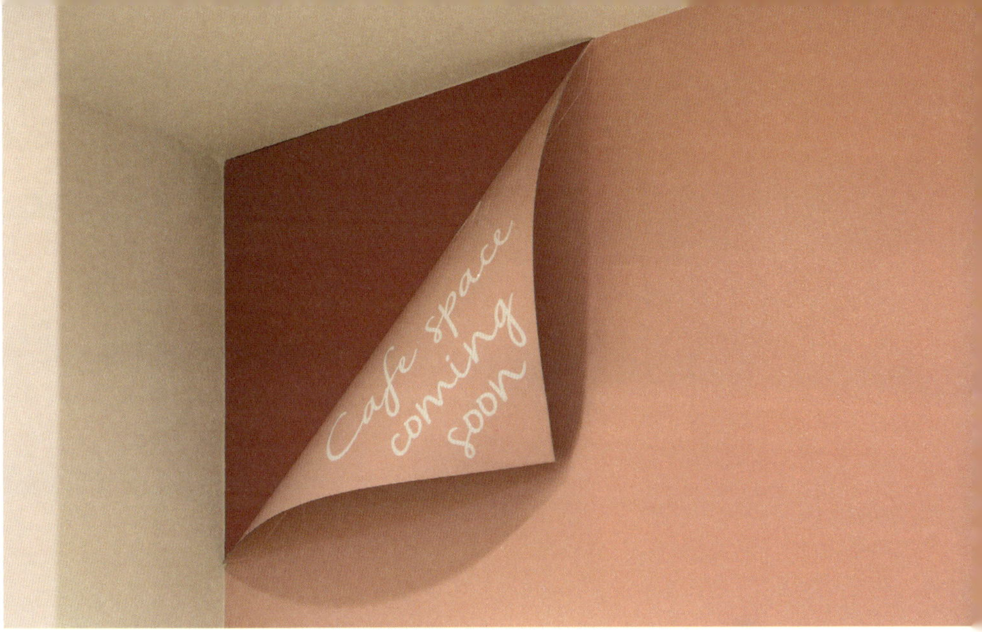
Cafe space
coming
soon

pâtisserie
Es-T

Yí PATISSERIE

SORABRAND

Huizhou, China

2153 square feet
(200 square meters)

2017

Yí Pâtisserie, founded in 2013, combines French baking, coffee, and Western-style light meals. With the brand slogan of "Joyful in every bite," the pâtisserie embraces the spirit of handmade French baking, which is to use with finest raw materials, and they wanted a design to reflect this.

The three-story duplex consists of a baking room, a simple dining room, a coffee shop, a tea room, and a logistic office space. Entering the space is like being surrounded by a European romance. Palace-style chandeliers hang from the ceilings of both the top and lower level. Copper and yellow light gently infuse the green marble workbench, which glitters with the various kinds of cakes in the glass display case. The wooden wall drips with Yi's trademark blue, which seems to flow like fresh milk.

The design group created large-scale floor-to-ceiling glass and structural metal frames to contrast against European-style architectural arched doors. The windows give a sense of light permeability for

customers, from inside and outside. The glass design also creates a subtle interaction between customers, while the frame design maintains the privacy of diners.

The French-romance-style hollow patio promotes communication between the floors and also works to unite them. With no partitions, the customers can communicate more freely in the space.

The overall brand vision was based on a French style, and the serif fonts and graphics combined with the exclusive "Yi's blue" became the logo. The combination of color vision, furniture color, and brand color is comfortable, natural, and relaxed. The brand illustration combined with brand positioning continuously convey the brand's internal appeal.

JOYFUL IN EVERY BITE.
CASHIER

JOYFUL IN EVERY BITE
PATISSERIE & CAFE

Temper Chocolate & Pastry

Evoke International Design

Vancouver, Canada

1400 square feet
(130 square meters)

2014

Awards: 2014 Outstanding Merit Specialty Food Retailer by A.R.E design award

Located in West Vancouver, the design requirement for this gourmet chocolate and pastry shop included allocating space for fully functioning chocolate and pastry kitchens while maintaining an inviting open retail experience.

The contemporary design was used to provide a clean and unadorned backdrop for the innovative quality of the chef's handcrafted products. Custom-glass display cases, natural materials, and linear lighting were used in order to achieve the bright, clutter-free layout of the space. An array of cut-off rolling pins and glass shelves were used to create a unique and functional display for the products. Windows in the wall separating the kitchen and retail spaces were added to the open concept, providing a view for customers to experience the process and specialty of the products being created on site.

Subtle accents were used to support the overall design concept: from the pendant lights chosen for their "pastry" aesthetic to

the custom wall covering with embedded light box and the custom-entry door pull branded with the client's logo. The fir-framed mirrors and art light box with original artwork enhanced the experience, bringing subtle graphic branding elements into the space.

The interior design utilized marble, mosaic tile, Douglas fir, and concrete to create a clean, contemporary interior. The glass display cases give prominence to the chef's artistic creations, while being integrated into the millwork and fixturing. The flooring was created from porcelain mosaic tiles. The combination of a European-style mosaic floor tile and a simple clean tile pattern marry classic European style with the contemporary aesthetic.

COFFEE
STUMPTOWN
ROASTERS

STUMPTOWN

EXIT
STARBUCKS COFFEE

Pâtisserie Alex

Union Atelier

Taipei, China

1561 square feet
(145 square meters)

2016

Pâtisserie Alex is a French dessert shop located in Taipei, China. The client sought to infuse a French elegance into the shop space and engaged Union Atelier to help them achieve this.

An airy sophistication was accomplished by introducing plenty of natural light into the interior. White was used as the primary tone, dotted with stylish colors, and the fine decoration of a board plays a key role in the whole space.

The external wall of the dessert shop was crafted using hues inciting a European atmosphere. A white three-dimensional signboard on the wall along with the golden words stuck on the glass highlight a sense of modest luxury. At the entrance, the design team placed a 23-foot-long (7-meter-long) counter and two glass showcases for cakes and used generous marble tabletops and copper European classical chandeliers to heighten the overall atmosphere.

Seats and counters were decorated in mint green, echoing the design emphasis of external walls. A long table that can accommodate 10 people was crafted, over which were installed unique glass drop lights to make this area a unique space where people can enjoy a nice afternoon with friends.

ALEX

ALEX

BLANCHIR

KOM Design Labo inc. (Jun Takagi + Moe Ishibashi)

Toyoyama-town, Japan

1518 square feet (141 square meters)

2016

This cake shop was named in honor of the very first bakery technique the owner learned—blanchir. The name reflects the owner's determination to not forget his original wish to vitalize his hometown of Toyoyama-cho, which is evident everywhere in the shop.

The interior décor subtly shows the dandelion imagery that stands for the magic of the blanchir technique to "whip to change the color from yellow to white." As blanchir is not a household word in Toyoyama, Japan, in order to convey what it means in a direct and easy-to-understand manner, the designers incorporated the fun and comprehensible elements into the interior design, such as the logo, original posters, and lighting fixture of the shape of mixing bowls.

The shapes and colors of the logo—how the cream is about to run from the bowl and the curves of letters—were carefully calculated to deliver the softness and "subtly mouth-watering" visual sensation.

Serving traditional confectionery, the design of Blanchir succeeded in revitalizing the owner's hometown through cakes.

BLANCHIR

BLANCHIR
なかよし山
¥130

BLANCHIR
ブランシール

Mélimélo

Daniela Arcila

Jalisco, Mexico

248 square feet
(23 square meters)

2018

Mélimélo is a Mexican and French pastry shop located in Zapopan, Mexico. Its name was derived from the French word "méli-mélo," meaning "combination" or "mix of two things," which well-befits this cross-cultural fusion.

Ana Karina, the owner, was born in Mexico but lived in the United States for half of her life and then travel to France, where she learned to bake as they do over there. As she wanted to project this combination of culture on her bakery, designer Daniela Arcila was engaged to create the interior and brand concept.

Melimelo's identity was highlighted by geometric patterns inspired by the most famous Mexican and French breads, for example, pan de muerto and baguettes. The blatant logo variation that was applied to the business cards represents the vibrant, carefree embodiment of the Mexican spirit that throws traditional conventions to the wind.

As part of the branding, the designer created different textures or patterns inspired in the elegance and folklore look of French and Mexican castle tiles. The bright and contrasting colors, combined with brushes of light pink and gold, were complemented by a touch of the sweet and contemporary. The blue would represent the old country, France; and the salmon touch the Mexican warm spirit.

The main typography selected for this project was inspired in the traditional touch of the "Lucha Libre's" (meaning "freestyle wrestling") posters, which had nothing to do with the brand, but were really popular in the Mexican culture.

The project was a challenge because the designer had only a week to develop the branding that could combine two completely different countries and cultures in a clean, subtle, and simple way.

MÉLI
MÉLO
Boulangerie
melimelo.com

MÉLI
MÉLO
Boulangerie
ANA KARINA ORELLANA

MÉLIMÉLO

MÉLIMÉLO
Boulangerie
MÉLI
MÉLO
Boulangerie
melimelo.com
ANA KARINA ORELLANA

cadeau de rincotté

KOM Design Labo inc.
(Jun Takagi + Mio Yoshida)

Kasugai-city, Japan

506 square feet
(47 square meters)

2013

Expanding on cadeau de rincotté's theme of "sweet gifts from nature," KOM Design Labo designed the interior space around the leitmotif of trees. Choosing mostly warm materials, the environment was further enhanced by panels made of straw to add a touch of playfulness.

Soft interior lighting was installed to evoke a gentle breathe of wind flowing through the space—all of which perfectly met the vision of the husband-and-wife owners for their cake shop.

The name of the shop, "rincotté"—a neologism composed by the owners by combining the name of their two children—and "cadeau de," which means gift, where taken into account when devising the logo for the store to represent the "gifts from nature" for sale. Thus, KOM Design Labo created an insignia of a tree growing from a gift box, which very clearly conveys their brand message.

To attract the attention of customers, rather than displaying the small baked

cakes in baskets or on plates, as in most shops, the design team came up with the idea of hanging them from hooks—just as a clothing store might hang socks—which further bolstered the nature theme, as the sweet packages are suggestive of leaves on a branch, as they're positioned before the tree silhouettes on the wall. Full of clever and humorous touches, the cake shop attracted many patrons.

リンコットの
オリジナル BOX
お好みのスイーツを入れて
ちょっとしたお礼に…
リンコットBOX
・マドレーヌ(2種)
・フィナンシェ
・クッキー(2種)
・ぽろん
計6個 ¥729
¥1100
¥857
cadeau de rincotte
http://rincotte.com/

ぽろん(黒糖) 大
¥389(税抜)
ぽろん(ごま・抹茶) 大
¥389(税抜)
ぽろん(きなこ) 大
¥389(税抜)
ぽろん(カシス)
¥389(税抜)
ぽろん(ベリー) 大
¥389(税抜)
ぽろん(スノー) 大
¥389(税抜)

ヘーゼルナッツ
いちご
カカオ
抹茶

¥416

コンフィチュール(ミルク)
¥500-
コンフィチュール(ミルクとあずき)
¥500-
コンフィチュール(抹茶)
¥550-
rincotté

春日井市出川町に、やさしさのつまったケーキ屋さん
8月1日(水)
GRAND OPEN!!
2日(木)も営業致します
商品売り切りにより閉店
とさせていただきます
はじめまして!
『自然からの甘い贈り物』
を届ける洋菓子店リンコットです。
2012年8月1日、愛知県春日井市出川町に洋菓子店「cadeau de rincotte(カド・ドゥ・リンコット)」がオープンします。
洋菓子に使われる自然素材＝「大地の恵み」を生かした上で、パティシエの手間ひまとアイデアで魔法をかける。
リンコットのケーキ達はそんなふうに出来た「自然からの甘い贈り物」です。あなたの身近な大切な人につい食べてもらいたくなる…そんなやさしさのつまったケーキ達をぜひご賞味ください!
リンコットのこだわり
rincotté
CLICK PLEASE
リンコット 春日井
rincotté
rincotté
rincotté
ぽろん(くるみ)
¥400-

しょうが
ココナッツ
トウモロコシ粉
バニラ

自然からの甘い贈り物
cadeau de
rincotté

Cafe Ki

id inc. (Seiji Oguri, Yohei Oki)

Tokyo, Japan

248 square feet
(23 square meters)

2017

Situated in Setagaya-ku, Tokyo, this coffee and pastry shop designed by Japanese id inc. provides a space where customers can enjoy a break within a small "forest."

Conceived in pure white, the palette works to enhance the structure of the "trees," which function as table legs, made of steel, and are tall enough to even hang hats and coats. Further, they allow a sense of comfortable distance for those sitting at the large shared table, as the wooden "branches" help to divide the space, while the overall "grove" works to amplify the entire space.

In addition to the interior design, id inc. was in charge of a variety of design elements, including naming, logo, shop card, menu, letter set, original font, and website. As Ki means "tree" in Japanese, a logo was composed of collected wooden branches, which was used throughout to give a soft and delicate impression with the brand consistency.

A series of original letter sets were creating using the tree motif. The original font was developed from the Ki logo, which was formed by collected wooden branches, and used for message cards, packages, and so forth.

Ki

珈琲とお菓子
ハンドドリップ (h/i)
カフェラテ (h/i)
カフェモカ (h/i)
フレーバーラテ (h/i)
紅茶（ディンブラ）(h/i)
自家製ジンジャーエール (h/i)
オレンジジュース
お菓子セット
480
450
480
450
950

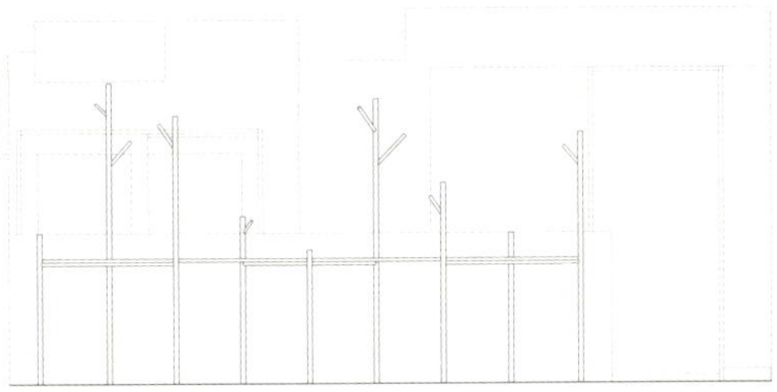

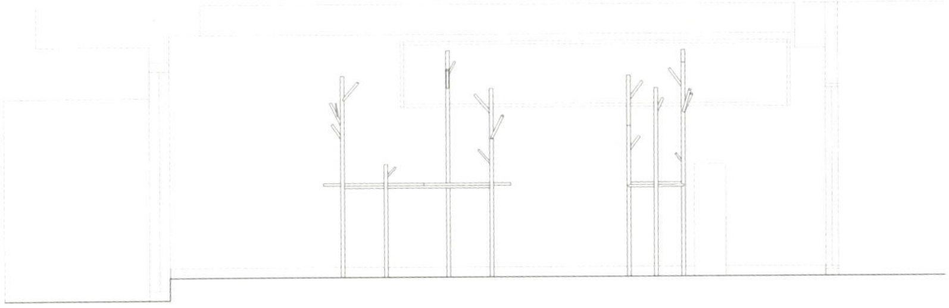

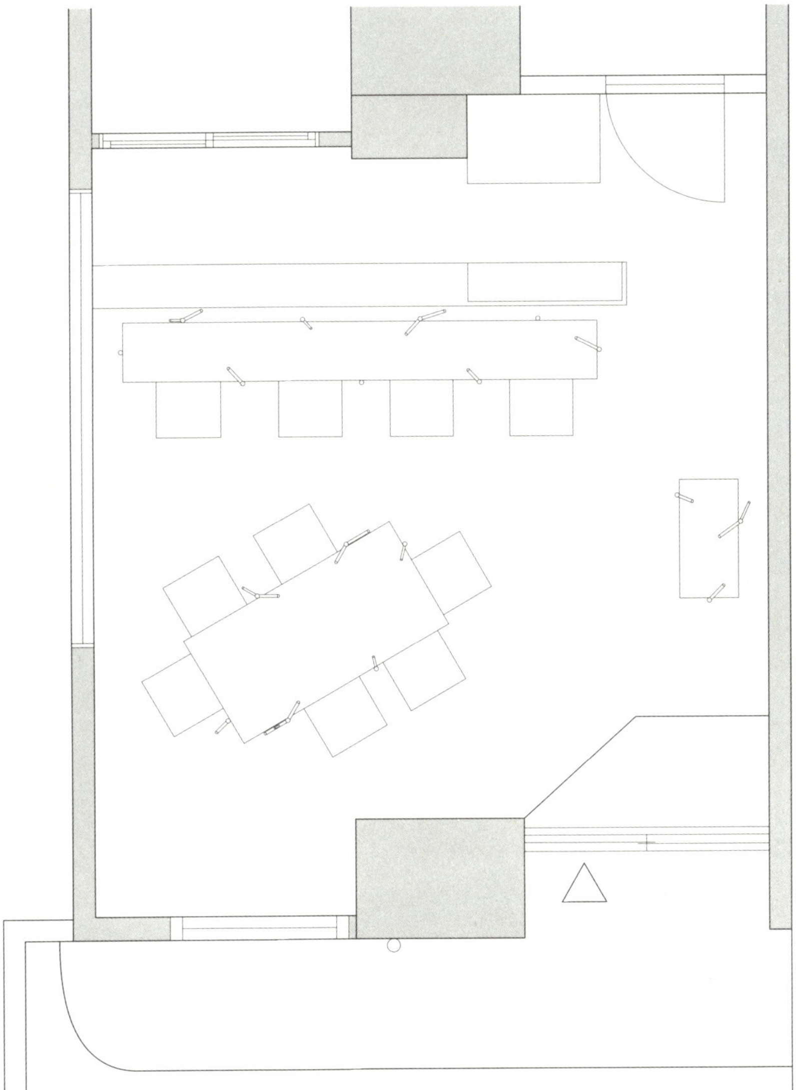

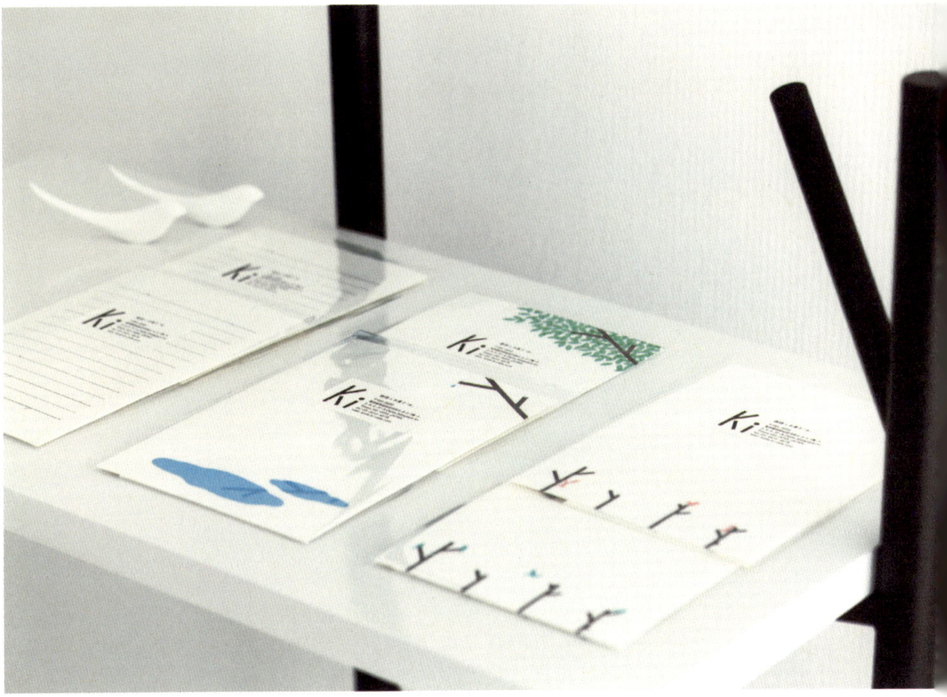
Ki
Ki
Ki
Ki
Ki

Citizen Sprout

Project M Plus

Santa Monica,
United States

360 square feet
(33 square meters)

2018

Jennifer Jewett created First Spoonful—a healthy solution for busy parents—as a way to meet the needs of families with little mouths to feed. She launched with a brilliant business plan and an impressive knack for home cooking. So delicious was her model that First Spoonful quickly outgrew its baby-centered focus and needed a new identity to appeal to a broader market as well as a brick-and-mortar storefront to support its fast-moving evolution.

Project M Plus supported Jennifer's vision, first with a naming exploration that conveyed her company's devotion to the health and well-being of both parents and their kiddos. Centered around family, Citizen Sprout needed a distinctively bright and lively personality to back its expansion into new markets with prepared home-cooked meals, treats, snacks, and nutritious lunch delivery to preschools and elementary schools throughout Los Angeles, California.

With a color palette of royals and periwinkles against pastel neutrals, Project M Plus landed on a playful script for the logo and designed a family of original illustrations. Adding layers to the brand experience, the packaging, print, and digital collateral rollout speaks a distinctively kid-friendly visual language.

Vinyl window graphics and illuminated signage boost their storefront curb appeal to capitalize on passing foot and auto traffic. Once inside, mod-style pendant lighting in mint, custom millwork retail shelving, a large-scale custom mural, easy-to-read menus, fun totes, and giveaway buttons work together for a curated brand experience. Add in a helping of vibrant photography and an intuitive e-commerce website and the consumer is offered an out-of-the-box experience that feels fresh, modern, and deliciously digestible.

OR A FAMILY.
Citizen Sprout
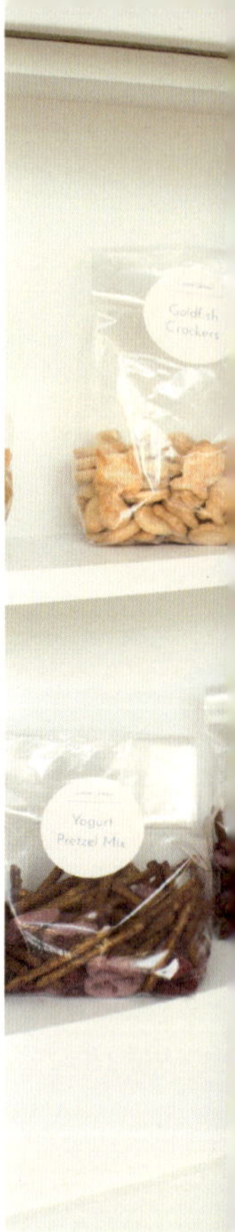
Yogurt Pretzel Mix

Citizen Sprout

Citizen
LOS ANGELES
Sprout

Casca

kissmiklos

Budapest, Hungary

463 square feet
(43 square meters)

2015

An artisan chocolate bar and café in Budapest, Hungary, Casca specializes in flavored and spiced chocolate bonbons and products made by the Kakas Bonbon factory, with coffee prepared by one of the best baristas and coffee specialist in Hungary.

Casca means "shell" in Portuguese—which is evocative of the beautiful shell-like appearance of their gourmet selection of bonbons on offer that have been likened to browsing the displays in an upscale jewelry store. As such, this delicate and delectable store needed some truly inspired branding.

When design company kissmiklos took over the project, a graphic design studio and an interior designer had already been working on its branding. kissmiklos created a new branding and redrew their logo—maintaining this primary focus of likening the products to precious gems. Additionally, with an initial theme established, kissmiklos was able to more easily harmonize the design of the interior

and graphics. While adapting the design to comfortably fit the space, kissmiklos also made the colors livelier and more integrated in the overall design.

Many subtle design details and gags were injecting into the space, such as a lamp and a wall console created from a tea jug and porcelain cup, while the chairs were selected in sync with the space and to be both comfortable and space saving.

CASCA
CHOCOLATE BAR & CAFÉ

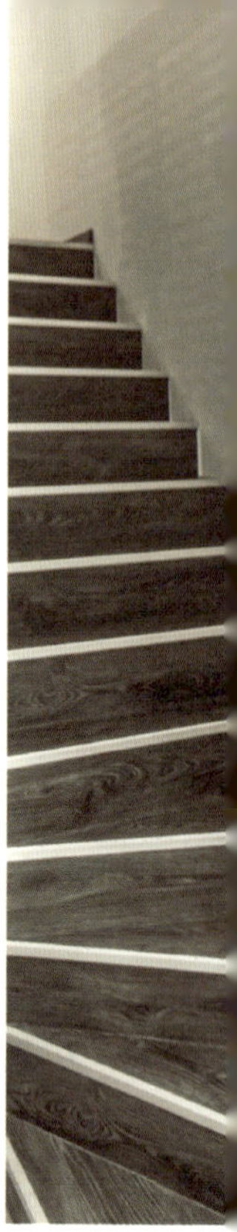

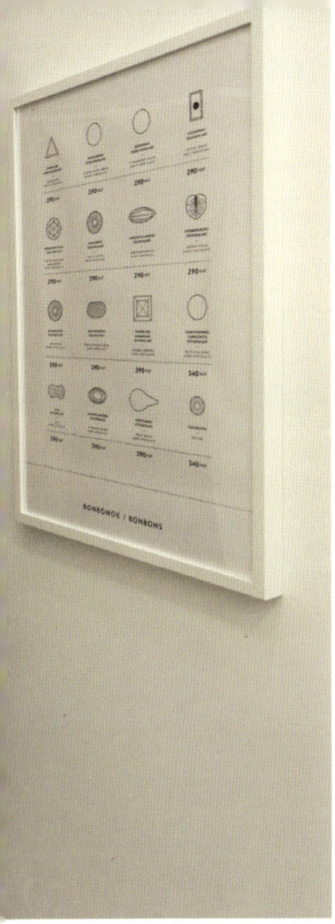

CAŠCA
CHOCOLATE BAR & CAFÉ

CAŠCA
CHOCOLATE BAR & CAFÉ

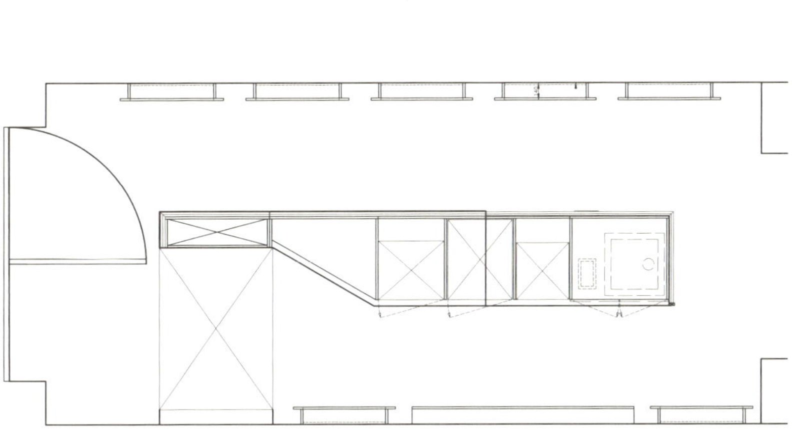

DON JUAN coffee & cakes

Vladimir Paripovic

Belgrade, Serbia

538 square feet
(50 square meters)

2016

On Resavska Street in the center of the Belgrade, a refreshed new concept for DON JUAN coffee & cakes was created by Vladimir Paripovic. Rebelling against the stone and concrete, gray tones and old façades of this famous city street, the cake shop sought to bring something special to cake and coffee lovers.

Designed in retro pink, white, and yellow with gold details, the colors worked to soften the straight lines of the space and create an environment where "magic happens," reminiscent of childhood. A whitewashed rustic timber floor that travels up the walls and a logo made seemingly of chocolate offer particular allure to visitors.

Aspiring to create interesting shadows and patterns, the design team chose to hang cakes on the window. Specially placed lighting was situated to illuminate the table and chairs and dozens of coffee cups were hung on the wall, casting a captivating silhouette across the entire space.

DON JUAN
coffee & cakes

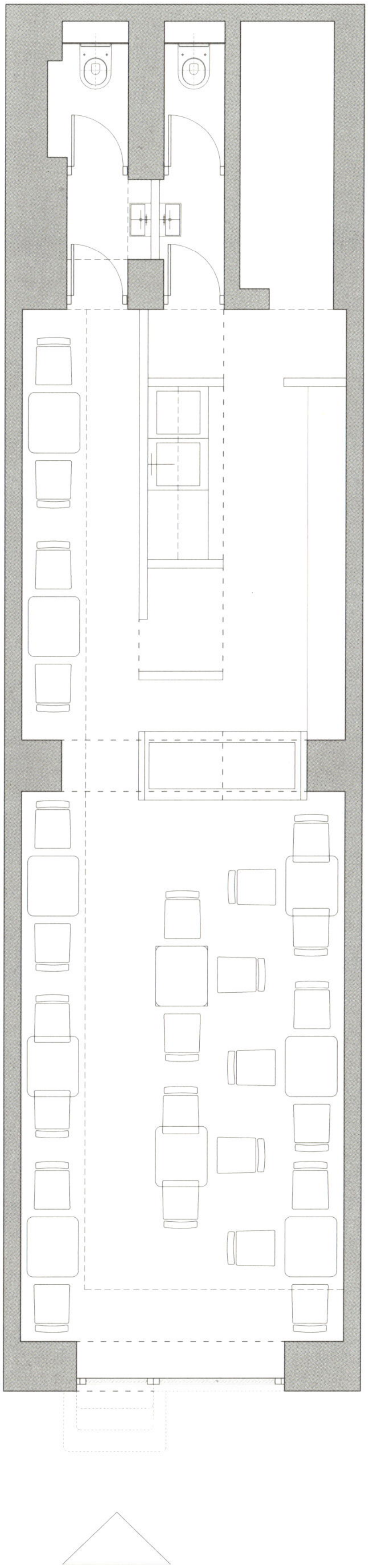

Julieta, Pan & Café

vitale

Castellón de la Plana, Spain

1076 square feet
(100 square meters)

2014

Where the protagonists of the space are bread and coffee, Julieta Pan & Café aspired to create café that was honest and simple with a respect for tradition, craftsmanship, and the dedication of a well-crafted product.

With these principles in mind, vitale designed the brand and the retail unit. The space was to have a dual function as both a bakery and coffee shop. Upon entry, customers are greeted by a long stone counter exhibiting the bread, pastries, and cakes. The brand values were transmitted by austere and simple materials like the cement counter, pine drawers pine for bread, and tiles, which evoke the appearance of traditional kitchens.

Beyond the counter is a café space for table services, backdropped by large windows that reinforce the friendly and transparent business spirit. This part of the establishment was created with homely materials and finishes, such as big armchairs, throw cushions, and soft furnishings to offer a warm and inviting atmosphere.

Lining the back wall, a long continuous bench was crafted of industrial wooden pallets and several cushions, and the four mobile tables provide great versatility for when clients need to adapt the distribution for a larger group. Succeeding in creating a relaxing and homely environment for customers to enjoy the products, the space can accommodate both intimate groups in cozy corners as well as bigger gatherings.

julieta
pan&café

El Moro

Cadena Concept Design

Mexico City, Mexico

8805 square feet
(818 square meters)

2015

The brand El Moro has been one of the most popular images of daily life in Mexico City since 1935, captivating a variety of audiences with its rich flavors, hot chocolates, and churros—claimed by some to be the best in the country's capital.

The guiding principle in the design of the project was in understanding their family values and history in order to merge them into a new strategic vision. Classic wall tiles became the main source of inspiration, along with stained-glass windows to backdrop the products that have set El Moro apart and delighted its customers for generations.

The new graphic system considered the figurative relationship between such elements and proposed a simplification in form, taking them to their minimalist expression to retain its essence but with a fresher and more dynamic form. This new take on endless compositional possibilities significantly enhanced the brand's identity, communication, architecture, and interior design. The chromatic palette, born from the

unmistakable mosaics that gave the brand its personality, were contrasted with a white hue inspired by sugar.

Language and furniture aligned, forming a unique expression reminiscent of the Golden Age in Mexico—when an Art Deco style dominated the city's poster ads, movies, fonts, and architecture—providing sufficient graphic elements, symbols, and even communication through different artistic means, thus creating a new integrated concept that emotionally connects people today with the collective subconscious in a new brand experience, which projects the true DNA of El Moro.

El
CHURRERO

CHURROS
CALIENTITOS
y
DELICIOSO
CHOCOLATE

CHURROS
Orden de 4 Churros $16
Mini Rosca $10
Dip de chocolate, cajeta o leche condensada $5
CHOCOLATE
Español - El tradicional, dulce y espeso $46
Mexicano - El más ligero $46
Francés - Con un toque de vainilla $46
Especial - Semiamargo con un toque de canela $52
Light - Sin azúcar y con leche light $52
Suizo - Con crema chantilly $52
Del Día - Pregunta por el sabor de hoy $52
PAQUETES
Chocolate Español + 4 Churros $60
Chocolate Mexicano + 4 Churros $60
Chocolate Francés + 4 Churros $60
Chocolate Especial + 4 Churros $66
Chocolate Light + 4 Churros $66
Chocolate Suizo + 4 Churros $66
Chocolate Del Día + 4 Churros $66
Malteada + 4 Churros $64
CONSUELOS
Consuelo $45
(Sandwich de mini rosca de churro con helado de chocolate, vainilla, fresa, oreo o helado del día)
Mini Consuelos (3) $45
El CHURRERO
EL MORO

CHURRERÍA
EL MORO
desde
1935

Sabah

Futura

Kuwait City, Kuwait

2018

With a menu ranging from donuts and handmade food to specially selected products from around the world, Sabah sells authentic sweets and savories to its Kuwaiti customers and international visitors.

The client reached out to Futura to create a close relationship between the brand and interior design, both of which were inspired by the aesthetics of the 1970s. Characterized by the use of organic and geometric shapes, pastel colors, and earthy tones that contrasted with brighter shades, other elements included the use of contrasting materials, such as wood and metal finishes.

The designers created a series of geometric patterns to be used in the different applications of the brand, such as coffee cups and coasters. The menu had a fun and original die cut, which merged perfectly with the playful and unique interior design.

As for the donut takeaway, the designers wanted to create something completely different to what was commonly used in

other bakeries: something fun that customers where happy to take with them—and even share on Instagram—and thus created individual half boxes of various colors with circular shapes symbolizing the donut within.

The designers paid great attention to the small details in the interior. Striving for a homelike and cozy feeling that invited customers to stay for a while, they also wanted a modern space with clean aesthetics evoking freshness and accessibility. The result was an oasis of comfort and fascinating interior design.

Thank you

Beverages
Breakfast

Enjoy!

SABAH
MENU
COFFE $ 13
DRINKS $ 25
BREAKFAST $ 22
LUNCH $ 12
PASTRY $ 19
COFFE $ 13
DRINKS $ 25
BREAKFAST $ 22
LUNCH $ 12
PASTRY $ 19
SABAH

Maruzen Tea Roastery

Lucy Alter Design, inc.

Shizuoka, Japan

1076 square feet
(100 square meters)

2018

Maruzen Tea Roastery, founded in Shizuoka Prefecture, celebrated its 70th anniversary in 2018. Lucy Alter Design was appointed to design the brand concept, product lineups, and the interior design, while also energizing the venerable shopping district of local Shizuoka.

Specialists in micro-roasting at high temperatures, the brand logo "° M" (Degree Maruzen) was created to communicate the temperature theme of the shop. A roasting studio was built within the shop for customers to taste and smell the products on offer.

On the first floor, the large curved bar counter offers a very eye-catching appeal, with a dining area on the second floor providing a long table to seat six. The interior space—including the bar counter, the tables, and chairs—was made predominately white to echo the logo and packaging of the brand.

The overall design style of the concept store followed a Japanese minimalist aesthetic.

The large floor-to-ceiling windows at the doorway provide an unobstructed view of the interior space to attract the attention of passersby, who can not only see the products within the store, but also watch the whole production process of the tea artist steeping leaves.

MARUZEN
Tea Roastery

MARUZEN
Tea Roastery

Tea Gelato & Drink Set
Single 850
Double 1,100
Tea Gelato
Single 450
Double 700
Affogato & Drink Set
Matcha Affogato 1,100
Brown Roasted Affogato 1,100
Genkotsu-ame 50
Drink
Hand-drip green tea 500
Gyokuro 600
Usuchatou (Latte) 500
Usucha arare (Latte) 500
Ryogouchi Bottling Tea 1,500

RL

Union Atelier

Taoyuan, China

1184 square feet
(110 square meters)

2016

Situated in Taoyuan, China, RL is a restaurant serving pastry and fine cuisine. Seeking a design with a subtle and stylish flair for their branding and interior, the design elements were ultimately decided to be as simple as the name—which is comprised of two letters.

The space was divided into two parts with a high contrast of black and white tones. The designers extended the materials from the ground to the ceiling with these two hues, creating, what they describe as a kind of "dark and bright mystery." As a result, the fascinating visual impact works to trigger customers' curiosity.

The left side of the space belongs to the pastry chef in shades of snowy white. Exquisite handmade French desserts are placed nicely inside the shiny showcase. By using white glossy tiles, white painted bricks, stainless finishing, and beautiful bright marble, the room is as elegant as the delicate desserts.

The right side of the space belongs to the cuisine chef where fine French burgers are served against a black backdrop. In order to create a powerful contrast within the space, the designers choose glossy black tiles, black painted bricks, blackened metal, and dark wood to not only try to create a conversation with the white space, but also to keep the space stylish.

Maison Marou Saigon

Rice Creative

Ho Chi Minh City, Vietnam

2314 square feet
(215 square meters)

2016

Maison Marou is a cafe, pâtisserie, and gourmet chocolate factory located in Ho Chi Minh City—a.k.a. Saigon—in Vietnam. Occupying a 1930s Art Deco building on Calmette Street in the heart of the city, the modern eatery offers contrast and hybridity within the bustling urban neighborhood.

For the design of the interior of Maison Marou, vertical rectangular units were repeated as a grid for the chocolate bar display. This unit is clearly visible at the "chocolate library," a major feature at the Maison, which showcases all of Marou's varied bars. Maison Marou is an experimental space where the chocolatiers can tinker and create new kinds of chocolate bars, bonbons, and pastries from local flavors on a weekly basis. For this reason, the designers created a movable system for the menu.

Marou's typeface was applied to chocolate-bar-shaped metal plates, which can be arranged and rearranged for the menu wall and the overhead signage. The letter forms

are also molded into small rubber pieces, which load into custom-made stamps for labeling all packaging and printed matter.

The design team found an important symbol (in Marou's own "Marou-mobile," a 1973 Vietnamese La Da Lat), which literally connects the cacao farms to the shop. The illustrated car often appears in the space and on packaging, tracing a line that the brand rides, between rugged and sophisticated. Uniforms at Maison Marou were inspired by the linen "jungle-shirts" that the Marou founders wore out in the field.

A flexible new set of brand elements played across the space. A rough illustration style expresses the rugged side of the brand, while a custom script draws inspiration from classic shop signage. The primary color palette bookends the well-known spectrum of Marou's origin-range chocolate bars. An additional green is sampled from the founder's iconic jungle shirts, while Marou's bright gold is an ever-present accent. Finally, the logo itself simply puts a roof over the Marou brand.

As Maison Marou required an ever-changing range of packaging, a flexible system was developed to apply across a plethora of shapes and sizes. Beyond packaged goods, the space welcomes the brand to create merchandise. The design elements give an unlimited amount of playful possibilities. Now able to share much more than just a packaged chocolate bar, the founders of Marou can fully express their spirit, and offer an experience steeped in cacao-collecting adventures and gourmet chocolatier know-how.

MAISON
SAÏGON
MAROU

WRAPPING
TEMPERING /
MOULDING

MAROU

35 GRAMMI

NINE associati

Frosinone, Italy

484 square feet
(45 square meters)

2018

NINE associati designed the first croissant cafè within the commercial area of Frosinone in Italy. Within the 484-square-foot (45-square-meter) space, color and branding were used to underline the strategic dualism of the client.

In Italy, consuming croissants and cappuccinos go hand in hand, so the request of the client was to create the first hybrid café in the city where the two could merge equally in the same "two-faced space." This became the starting point for the brand identity and the interior design.

Within the concept of this duality of the croissant and cappuccino, paired with the notion of this being a space to take a moment to recharge, relax, and socialize from morning to night, the designers came up with a contrasting color theme of soft teal and stark white split right down the middle of the interior. This both enlivens the space and gives an illusion of it being wider. The furnishings were designed by NINE associati and tailor-made by local companies to blend with the space while the graphics on the wall and printed on the packaging provide visual continuity.

cos'è il caffè?
Il caffè è una
scusa.
Una scusa per dire a un
amico che gli vuoi bene."

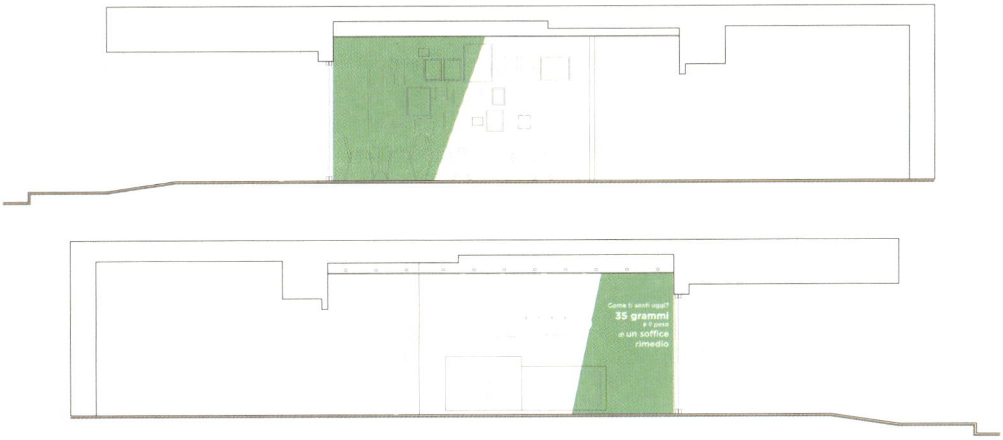
35 grammi
un soffice
rimedio

cos'è il caffè?
scusa.

35 grammi

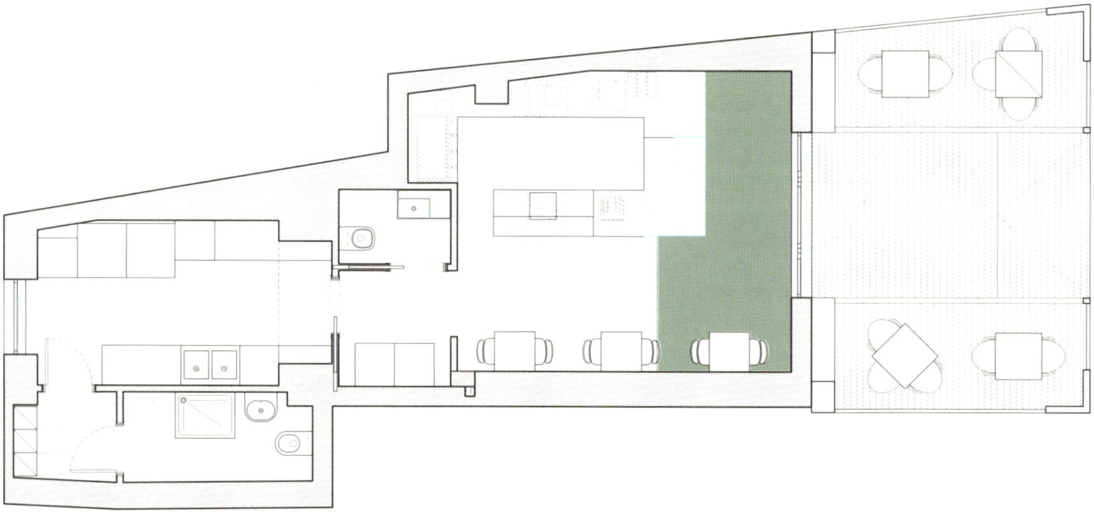

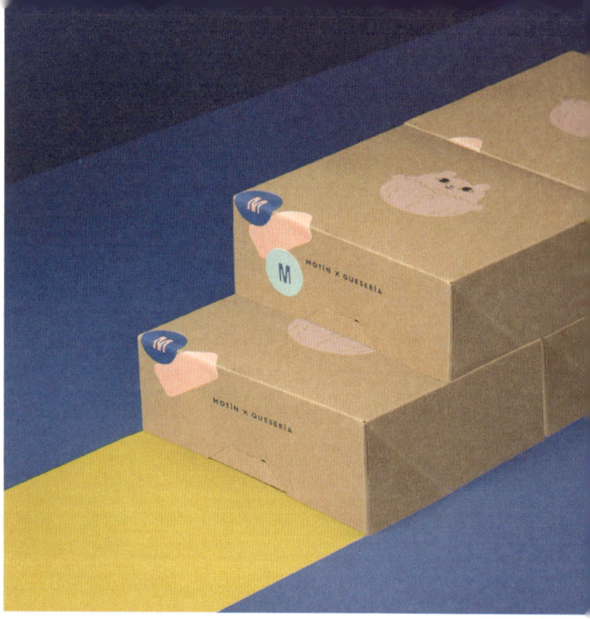

Motín

Futura, Solvar

Mexico City, Mexico

807 square feet
(75 square meters)

2019

Motín is an all-day café located in Colonia Roma, one of the trendiest neighborhoods in the culinary scene of Mexico City. Futura was in charge of the naming and branding, while local studio Solvar executed the interior design.

Within an 807-square-foot (75-square-meter) space situated in what was previously an end-of-19th-century house with classical French-style architecture—typical of the Roma and Condesa neighborhoods—the area was integrated into a mixed-use project with offices and commercial premises that respected the original façade. Motín was installed in what were the common areas of the old residence, with direct access from the street.

With a focus on delicious plates of food—some naughty, some healthy, and all mouthwateringly divine—the space was created to invite customers in with its cozy pink and blue palette and a gluttonous hamster brand identity with eyes bigger than its stomach. The space entices

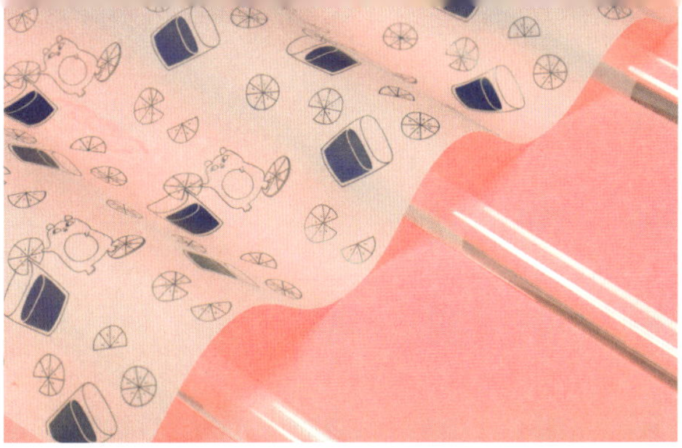

customers to enjoy some sweets or a cup of coffee while doing some work on a Monday morning, or to share a plate of fluffy pancakes at weekend brunch in this fun-loving environment that doesn't take itself too seriously.

Maui Pops

Brandon Archibald

Hawaii, United States

1184 square feet
(110 square meters)

2017

Part of a popsicle chainstore located on the island of Maui in Hawaii, Brandon Archibald was engaged to develop a brand concept and identity of Maui pops, including the interior design of the shop.

As the designers started working on the project and exploring the task, they were attracted by a quintessentially Hawaiian character—the tiki. In Polynesian culture, tikis are different types of idols ranging from wooden ceremonial statues of Māori tribes to the stone figures on Easter Island. Hawaiian culture has the same roots. For that reason Brandon Archibald decided to use the tiki as a key branding element.

The branding was developed along with the interior design—the core idea was a mixture of ethnic motives in a contemporary look and a colorful palette that suits the bright Hawaiian spirit. The style started growing into something fun—new moves, fonts, and other graphic solutions were added.

The main character, the tiki, was positioned to meet customers inside the shop. He is a part of a phrase that combines words with symbols. The designers added juicy fruit signs that demonstrate the variety of popsicle flavors. And the exit was positioned through the gift shop for additional marketing potential. The designers made three heights of chairs for the kids of different ages and grownups. The counter complements the chairs and makes the interior more dynamic.

GIFT SHOP
t-shirt 12
snapback 10
eco bag 10
sunglasses 6
my bottle 8
notebook 4
diary 4
stickers 2
magnets 3

GIFT SHOP
maui pops

HERE YOU CAN TASTE DELICIOUS
maui POPS
MADE
OF NATURAL INGREDIENTS THAT GROW UNDER
BRIGHT HAWAIIAN AS FOR
HE LIKES
AND POPSICLE THE MOST
ALOHA

maui
POPS
TIKI
BOOM

MANGO TANGO
#2 NANA MOU
#3 LANI KAI
POMAIKA'I
NOKEO
FIGGIN AWESOME
AKAMAI
1,5 $

THE
maui

ZERO-e ice cream café

NINE associati

Isola del Liri, Italy

409 square feet
(38 square meters)

2017

Creating ice-cream for over a century, the Masci family has been preserving and handing down the craft secrets related to Italian ice-cream traditions since 1898. Situated in the old town center of Isola del Liri, ZERO-e was established to be the first "clean label" ice-cream café in the district, as well as the first café to propose a culinary experience around ice-cream.

Italian architecture firm NINE associati created a fully tailor-made interior for ZERO-e. The interior of the shop, from the graphics on the walls down to the smallest accessories, as well as all the company branding, was completely designed by NINE associati and manufactured by local Italian artisans.

The project was propelled by the need to renew the 409-square-foot (38-square-meter) impersonal space in a very short time, while also equipping it with a kitchen, so the strategy was broken into three objectives: optimization of the interior, tailor-made design of the furniture, and

flexible use of spaces over time. These points were strictly linked and the whole design concept was born from the perfect balance between them.

A series of minimal architectural changes removed any blind spots and provided flexibility for the positioning of technical equipment, and also adapted the space to the different customer flows during the year. Everything in the room—tables, stools, shelves, etc. including the coating of technical elements—was designed to optimize both the functionality and the visual perception of the spaces. The open-view warehouse boxes and two large magnetic walls were the key elements of the main hall, characterized by the seasonal and daily changing of colored elements standing out against the light-blue background. A sliding window worked to open the small room towards the main square of the city.

Graphic communication, interior architecture, and furniture design were melted together, letting the space interact with both the interior and exterior while communicating the scale of the story and the owners' philosophy, even when the café is closed.

DIAMO IMPORTANZA A QUELLO CHE NON C'E'!
SENZA ADDENSANTI E EMULSIONANTI
VEGANO
SENZA LATTOSIO
IPOCALORICO

NATURA
QUALITA'
PASSIONE

ZERO

TIRAMISU
MELONE

ZE
RØ

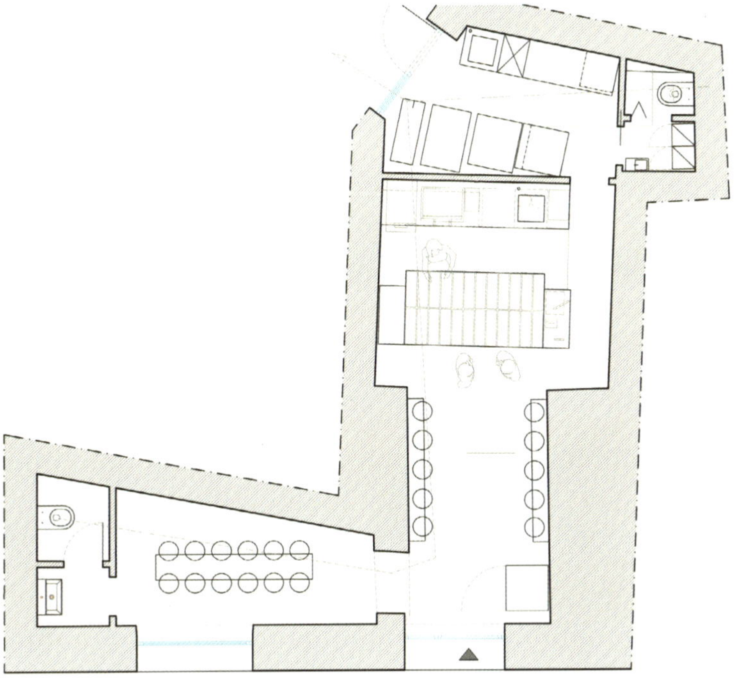

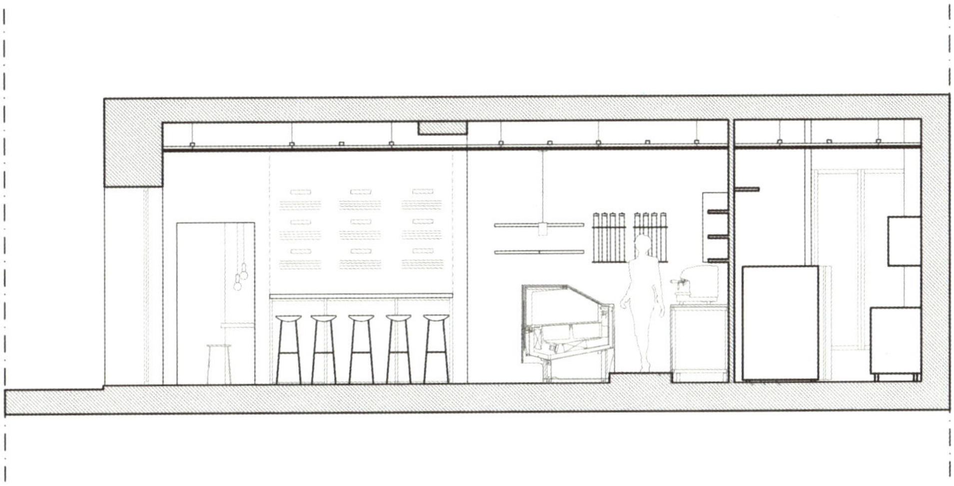

Prossima Fermata—ice cream laboratory

studio wok

Milan, Italy

172 square feet
(16 square meters)

2018

Curzio Baraggi, the master ice-cream maker of Prossima Fermata, imbues value into the products that he make with his incredible skills. He also invites the public to assist in the preparation of the ice-cream, thus making them fully aware of what they are eating to further promote the pure and natural philosophy of the store.

As such, studio wok took into account Baraggi's attentiveness and scientific approach to creating his ice-creams, and the design team focused on the concept of "ice-cream workshop"—merging sales and hands-on manufacturing. The architecture, consequently, had to accommodate this while also providing a coherent retail space in itself.

There were three key features of the renovation: a burgundy-colored "swimming pool" floor, a monolithic counter, and the reorganization of a group of refrigerators. Three natural materials were used: linoleum, stone, and wood. A section of the walls and floor were covered with burgundy

linoleum, marking a kind of colorful pool linking the workshop with the shop space. This material change highlighted the counter and minimized the technical and functional layers. The ice-cream counter, with a square and monolithic shape faced in stone, provided a simple material with traditional values.

The protagonists of this ice-cream store—the 24 flavors—were printed on cards and framed on the wall to give a brief description of the flavor, possible allergens, the nutritional table, and whether it's lactose based, vegan, or sorbet. The effect of this is both informative to customers while also projecting the wholesome and natural theme of the ice-creamery that aspires to create new taste experiences and develop every product to its full potential.

SORBETTI SU STECCO
CHIEDICI I GUSTI
PERA
OPUNZIA
CARAMELLO SALATO
MERINGATA E ARANCIA ROSSA
PISTACCHIO PURO DI STIGLIANO
TORRONE
MANDARINO
MANGO
ARANCIA ROSSA
FIORDILATTE
TIRAMISU
CANNELLA E ZENZERO
CREMA STREGATA
LIMONE
KIWI
CIOCCOLATO FONDENTE
ZUCCA ALLA MANTOVANA
STRACCIATELLA
LIQUIRIZIA
PASTA DI MANDORLA

GRANITA AL CARCADÈ
PERA
MERINGATA E ARANCIA ROSSA
Meringhe con succo di arancia rossa
SORBETTO
OPUNZIA
Opuntia Dillenii, Salento
GELATO
GRANITA ALLA MANDORLA
GRANITA ALLA FRAGOLA
ARANCIA ROSSA
FIORDILATTE
TIRAMISU
CANNELLA E ZENZERO
Piccante, non per tutti!
CREMA STREGATA
Crema delicata aromatizzata anche con il liquore Strega
GRANITA AL LAMPONE
GRANITA AL FICO
CIOCCOLATO FONDENTE
Sorbetto di cioccolato con massa di cacao
ZUCCA ALLA MANTOVANA
Zucca e amaretti
STRACCIATELLA
Con panna, latte fresco della Valtellina e cioccolato fondente
LIQUIRIZIA
TORTA PAESANA

Kinber Made

Filter017 / Wen

Taichung City, China

1421 square feet
(132 square meters)

2018

Founded in Taichung City in 2014, Kinber Made sought to be an industry leader and set trends with their creative ice-cream made of natural ingredients while aspiring to provide a different experience for their guests.

Focused on creating spaces that blend the delicacy of the product with a passion for literature and art, in the spring of 2018, Kinber Made opened a new shop with the concept of "The Sense Guide Parlor," selling creative ice-creams as well as delicate desserts, coffee, and drinks.

The shop—located in a Japanese-style courtyard on Jingcheng 5th Street—retained the original structure and charm of the old house. A hint of industrial roughness and the delicacy of Nordic and Japanese styles were integrated into the overall space to create a comfortable environment.

Filter017 / Wen, a well-known design team in Taiwan, designed a new visual image for Kinber Made in additional to creating a composite show space on the second floor of the shop and a concept unit "TPR" (The

Parlor Room), which could be used to sell small items related to life, design, and art, and to display works from artists, designers, and art groups occasionally.

BASIC
COMBO
小聖代 MINI
SNACK
DRINK
CASHIER

Softsrve Ice Cream & Dessert Bar

Wil Ken

Petaling Jaya, Malaysia

1650 square feet (153 square meters)

2015

Undertaking the entire branding of Softsrve, both the client and designer sought a bold, yet minimalistic, identity for Softsrve—an ice-cream and dessert bar situated in Petaling Jaya, Malaysia—that melded the branding, graphics, and interior.

One of the initial issues that the designer faced upon commencement of the project was the annoying echo in the space, which was common in many shops in Kuala Lumpur. As the commercial shop lots are long and narrow, the problem of an echoing interior space is almost unavoidable and Softsrve's interior was no different, which was very disrupting. As such, left-over carpet tiles from the contractor were installed underneath each table as a means of absorbing some of the echo.

In terms of design, solid pine wood and pine veneer were selected to complement the all-white space, with a main counter exposed and relaxed to allow harmony between the customer and staff. Crafted at a user-friendly height that maintains an openness

with the rest of the interior, the materials selected were white ceramic tile topped with solid pine.

A long pine shelf fixed to the wall was used to hold a myriad of glass jars, paper cups, and the ice-cream menus in frames. All the bar stools were purchased by the client and were carefully selected to match the design of the interior in all white and pine.

The dining wall was deliberately left bare as part of the minimalist statement, with an off-white curtain hung at the back wall to conceal the workings of the kitchen in the rear, thus limiting the customers' vision to only the white and warm interior of the shop. A simple render of cement for the floor was the single contrast in the otherwise warm and white-washed interior. To top it off, a neon sign was positioned on a feature wall bearing a quirky tagline "Go soft or go home."

ICE CREAM & DESSERT BAR

Winter Milk

Anagrama

Monterrey, Mexico

689 square feet
(64 square meters)

2017

An ice-cream shop located in Monterrey, Mexico, Winter Milk is characterized by its wide variety of fresh lactose-based products, handcrafted with 100 percent natural ingredients, with ice-cream cones, popsicles, milkshakes, frappes, and desserts among the offerings on their menu.

With 16 locations, the concept for this shop sought to create a traditional atmosphere and uplifting experience for enjoying and sharing ice-cream with family and friends. The graphic identity centered on employing different typographies reminiscent of the graphical hand-made labeling and signs of cafeterias from the 1960s. The result comprises a compendium of custom-made logos for the brand collateral and store interiors.

The color palette reflects a combination of warm oranges and fresh blues. The orange gradation references the emblematic traditional color of the Dutch monarchy, while the blues were used to resemble the winter and cold climates. The overall effect

offers a bold, distinctive, and instantly recognizable brand identity for the ice-cream label.

MR. PISTACHIO
COOKIE MONSTER

PROPERTY OF
WINTER MILK™
ICE CREAM
· Frozen Desserts · Coffee ·
SCOOP UP SOME ORIGINAL WINTER FLAVOURS
CRAFTSMANSHIP

WINTER MILK

ICE CREAM
Wintermilk

ICE CREAM
WINTER
MILK

HELADOS
SENCILLO
DOBLE
LITROS
CONO $32
VASO $32
WAFFLE BOWL $37
CONO $52
VASO $52
WAFFLE BOWL $57
450 ML. $62
1 LT. $129
PALETAS
DE LA CASA $24
ESQUIMAL $29
ESQUIMAL + TOPPING $34
FRAPPÉ
FRAPPUCCINO
FRAPPE MOCHA
12 OZ
16 OZ
OREO
SNICKER BLAST
MALTEADAS

WINTER MILK
EXTRAS

ICE CREAM
WINTER
MILK

Milk Land

Ryusuke Nanki, Hiroki Segawa

Tokyo, Japan

463 square feet
(43 square meters)

2018

Situated in Tokyo, Milk Land was created to promote the dairy products of Hokkaido, where more than half of Japan's dairy products are produced. Originally a pop-up store, the design of the space worked as a giant advertisement for the products.

Attracting people with bold cow print, the designers used this theme throughout to promote the brand. The shop was designed so as to create synergy between eating and the dairy farm, leading to effective building on the brand.

"We thought of this place as an advertising space where people could walk in to sample the products," said designer Ryusuke Nanki. The giant billboard with cow print attracts the attention of passersby, drawing people into the shop, which is also fully covered from floor to ceiling with black-and-white bovine spots.

At the ice-cream counter (also covered in cow print), customers can buy soft-served ice-cream or sweets made from milk and head to the floor above. The cow pattern

continues on to this floor where a life-size model of a cow blends in with the black-and-white pattern. Beside it, a large toppings bar awaits for customers to choose their own combinations of fixings for their sweets.

The semi-elliptical toppings bar appeared as if it had risen up from the floor with the same familiar cow pattern. This bar was made from the same materials as the walls and the floor, making the various kinds of colorful toppings in the containers stand out. Some of the toppings' containers, by using air pressure, pop up like moles in Whack-a-Mole, adding fun and delight to the customers' experience.

夏だって
生乳を
ていねいに
搾ったら
TOPPING
COUNTER
MILK LAND KITCHEN

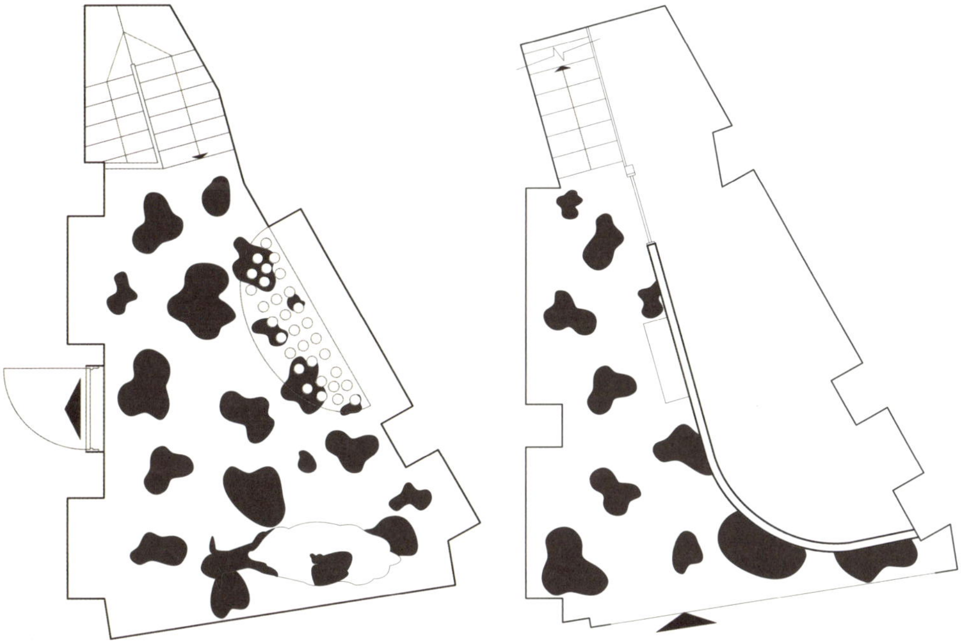

MILK
LAND
Hokkaido

Spooning Cookie Dough Bar

Zentralnorden

Berlin, Germany

237 square feet
(22 square meters)

2017

For the growing food brand Spooning, Zentralnorden created the first of several cookie dough bars to sell raw dough to customers, which was previously unheard of in Germany. Located in Berlin's popular Prenzlauer Berg, the design team transformed a narrow, dark 237-square-foot (22-square-meter) front space into a bright and playful journey into everybody's childhood of nibbling raw cookie dough in grandma's kitchen.

With a very small budget, the designers used a mixture of graphic color zones in pink, white, and dark blue combined with very classic white tiles for wall coverings. The bar was kept very simple with an 11-foot (3.3-meter) freestanding center desk to present the 10 different mixes of cookie dough and a variety of well-selected toppings. Children are able to use the bright-yellow handle bar to climb one step up to see what's in the dough-filled bowls.

In order to spread the word about the new place on social media, they added some arty installations like a "forget your diet" neon

sign on a dark-blue wood panel, a shuttlecock arrangement, and a menu board behind the desk with changeable hand-stamped letters on pieces of plywood.

Also, the light concept was kept very graphic by using regulable LED tube lights, which were arranged closer in the back and wider in the front of the bar to give more visual depth to the room. All furniture was made of a combination of coated steel and glazed plywood. To make the look more graphic, every part of the furniture in front of the pink wall was also covered in the same shade of pink.

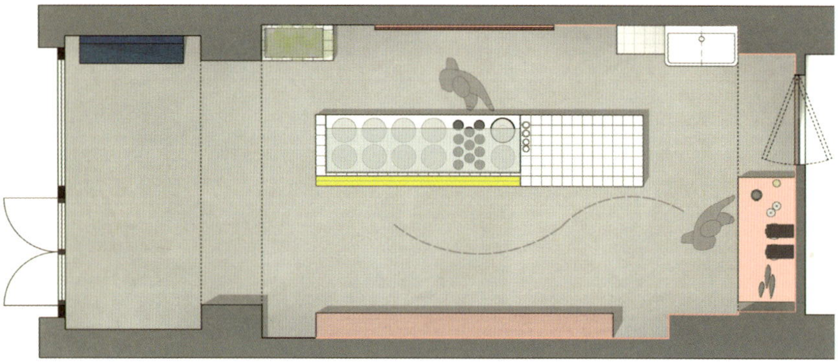

#fuck
your
diet

SPOONING

HOW IT WORKS
FORGET YOUR DIET
WAHLE DEINE SORTEN
WAHLE DEINE TOPPINGS
TOPPING +0.50
COFFEE & DRINKS → MENU

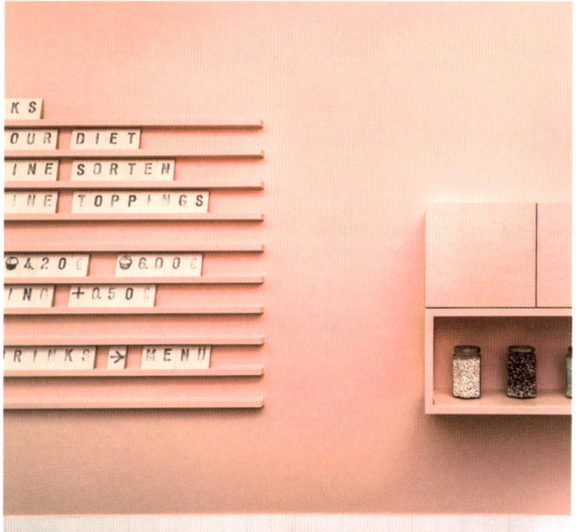

Choya Ume Specialty Shop

Lucy Alter Design, inc.

Kyoto, Japan

355 square feet
(33 square meters)

2018

Specialists in high-quality plum products, Choya Ume in Kyoto, Japan, appointed LUCY ALTER DESIGN, inc. to complete a brand design that extends from concept and interiors to the product lineup. The design began by installing large French windows displaying the whole interior space of the store to passersby, who can see the internal decorations and products very clearly. Two natural-colored benches in front of the door allowing seating for customers who want to enjoy the outdoors when the weather is nice.

The overall design of the store was based on a minimalist style. The design team chose white as the main tone, which works in harmony with the brand's packaging. The long white bar was positioned in the middle of the space and echoes the wood-colored cabinets and cutlery. As the main area of the product display, the design team placed glasses filled with plums and Konpeitō (sugar candy) along the walls so that the product packaging could also be regarded as a part of the design.

Choya Umeshu Co., Ltd was founded as a grape farm and started manufacturing umeshu (plum liqueur) in 1959. They have since been striving to improve their products and technological innovation to improve the quality. While Lucy Alter designed the brand concept, product lineups, and the interior design, they also redesigned the Japanese plum culture for the next generation.

Hailing from a tradition of harvesting the fruit from your grandmother's garden in the rainy season and making umeshu—a process involving picking plums from a branch, putting them in a basket, washing them, putting them in a bottle, and soaking them in ice sugar—inside the store, customers are able to choose their favorite ingredients from carefully selected materials (five kinds of plum, five kinds of sugar, and four kinds of sake) and add their own syrup to craft their own plum wine.

Reminiscent of a warm tradition in Japanese culture, customers are reminded of the past when their mothers or grandmothers used to make the sweet liqueur and their fathers got to drink it! All of these factors were valuable in the design process.

Jayde's Market

Project M Plus

Los Angeles, United States

6360 square feet
(591 square meters)

2018

A few short years ago, baby Jayde was born to the ambitious Plejer family. Unbeknownst to her, a thoughtfully designed marketplace would soon open in her namesake.

"We approached the owner about making substantial changes to the existing building to reimagine how the patron uses the space," said principal architect and co-founder at M Plus, McShane Murnane. "We created a new entry point modeled after a greenhouse that gives an uplifting first impression and sets the tone for the whole market."

Entering via the full-glass ceiling atrium, shoppers can stop in for a coffee and fresh pastry, mingle with neighbors, or enjoy a sunny respite before filling their basket with thoughtfully selected staples and international fare. In order to let the market breathe, M Plus took this dark, dilapidated strip mall store and brought the light in with skylights, layered pendants, and designed light-box signage

to illuminate way-finding—all modeled after small, curated, urban European markets, which you just can't find anywhere else in Los Angeles.

Conceived around the ethos of a neighborhood market, Jayde's was designed to feel like an extension of the upscale homes in the area. A café and flower shop await in the annex, where porcelain herringbone flooring, white oak paneling, galvanized flower vases, and brass finishes lend a distinctly European flair. Custom white-oak shelving within the market nods to a sophisticated farmhouse feel. Quotes from renowned chefs grace the transparent freezer doors for inspiration.

M Plus' signature whimsy leads visitors up to Jayde's Bottle Shop, an intimate lofted wine room. Custom mosaic tiles greet shoppers in several languages, setting a celebratory tone on the way to Jayde's sommelier who is always on hand to help explore a finely curated selection of wine and spirits.

Nestled in the hills just off Mulholland drive, Jayde's now fills a once conspicuous gap in convenience and epicurean experience that brings community together to celebrate food and friendship.

VERVE
VERVE

EXIT

Ground, dripped,
steamed, iced,
brewed, milked,
baked, melted,
buttered, ready to
chase the day.
JAYDESMARKET.COM

FIJI

TARTINE BREAD

JAYDE'S

CAFE
EXIT

The
BOTTLE
SHOPPE
L'CHAIM!
SALUD!
NA ZDROWIE!

CAFE

HI-LO Liquor

Project M Plus

Culver City, United States

1600 square feet
(149 square meters)

2014

From affordable Kentucky whiskeys to small-batch wines and seasonal cult beers—along with a revolving selection of uniquely curated goods, such as fruit products, sausages, dairy products, snacks, many frozen treats, and heritage sundries—the branding of HI-LO Liquor in Culver City, needed more acute defining.

The owners, Chris and Talmadge, approached Project M Plus for collaboration in redesigning the physical space. The goal was to make the interior and brand of HI-LO Liquor fashionable to the everyman and the connoisseur alike.

Embracing the contrasts and contradictions, Project M Plus created a European storefront with a slightly more bold and elevated design in striking red with a confident typeface, which juxtaposes against the very pared-down, utilitarian interior that iterates Hi-Lo's literal purpose.

Brass-gilded sconce and mail-slot details added classic layers, while hand-painted

signage doles out a helping of earnest humility. Greeted by the tiled-in motto, “Drink Well,” guests immediately feel the shop’s pragmatic modernity while its airy, exposed white beams keep the space open and fresh.

MARKET GOODS
SALTY
TEQUILA & MEZCAL
VODKA & GIN

DRINK GOOD BEER.

HI-LO
HI-LO
DRINK WELL
COOL FOOD.

Hi—Lo
Liquor Market
HI—LO

Abarrotes Delirio

Savvy Studio
Mexico City, Mexico
2013

Abarrotes Delirio is an old-fashioned-style general store located in the Roma Norte neighborhood in Mexico City selling carefully selected produce, freshly baked bread, prepared foods, local jams, honeys, wines, and other special treats complemented by a window outside serving up coffees, desserts, and the tortas for those wanting a quick gourmet fix.

The design objective was to communicate Abarrotes Delirio's philosophy—based on practicality, simplicity, and the organic provenance of their ingredients—through its identity and interior design. Aspiring to counterpart local life and healthy eating with its authentic, specialized, and practical offerings, the design requirement was to marry the new gastronomic culture that mixes street food with gourmet food into their pantry-like setting.

The contrast between the opposing concepts of a corner shop and a gourmet one was resolved by Savvy Studio through a neutral and pristine interior able to amplify the

colors of the products. Flexible signage—with both static and adjustable options—allowed the versatility of being adaptable to the always-changing product offerings, which were also depicted in the graphic style developed for the brand.

The practicality and informative nature of the space and the branding sought to express a warm and inviting essence, to represent a simple and tranquil refuge with a great selection of food that adds value to routine.

Baguette
Ciabatta
$15

Manzanilla
Bugambilia
Sencha
Rooibos
Verde
Marroquí
Infusiones
Vaso desechable
12 oz.
Fajillas
P/ vaso

LUNES
9am

PANADERÍA
DELIRIO
Campesino Rústico
Campesino con Aceitunas
Integral & Ciabatta

QUESOS
Semiduro de Oveja, Gruyère,
Mozarella Fresco, Gorgonzola,
Ramonetti Doble Crema,
Chihuahua, Real del Castillo,
Brie & Camembert
Selección de pequeños productores,
en su mayoría nacionales.
ABARROTES
DELIRIO
ABARROTES
DELIRIO

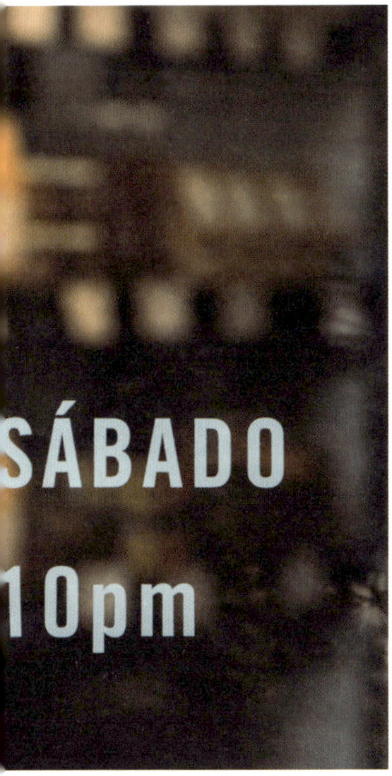
SÁBADO
10pm

Kostarelos

STIRIXIS Group

Athens, Greece

1055 square feet
(98 square meters)

2015

Awards: Build Architecture Award for Best Greek F&B Project 2016; Best Retail Interior Europe at the International Property Awards 2016–2017

Since 1937, Kostarelos has been producing fine cheeses and dairy products. The flagship store in Kolonaki, Athens, was holistically designed by STIRIXIS Group and constitutes the evolution of the retail chain into a distinctive Greek delicatessen that combines both a shop space selling Greek delicacies and the sit-in experience of enjoying specialty dishes made of Kostarelos's products. The store perfectly matches those two areas, both conceptually and in terms of design.

The STIRIXIS Group design team created a beautiful, cozy environment of unique style with details that highlight the company's values and heritage—from the stunning wall covered with wooden pieces of the actual beech barrels that the company used for the cheese aging in their factory and the big pendant lights that resemble the metal hoops of those barrels to the floor tiles that make a strong reference to the Greek flag color palette. A new wall-covering graphic pattern for the food area was also

composed, formed by icons reminiscent of cheese, cold cuts, wheat, and the plaid of traditional Greek tablecloths.

The pattern and the way it was applied in the store in combination to other branding applications, like the packaging, and in-store communication, looks like it is embroidered rather than graphically designed. Additionally, the blackboard used for the menu was coherent with the overall brand strategy of creating a contemporary and traditional style.

All menu suggestions were prepared with products from the family's own cheese factory and other products

City

and ingredients carefully selected from Greek artisan producers that can be found at the store's grocery. Upon entering, customers are introduced to the pleasures of authentic Greek flavors in a welcoming environment that delivers a special and memorable store experience.

Truly supporting its holistic approach, beyond the architectural and branding design of the new store, STIRIXIS Group provided a wide set of services for the overall development of the brand, such as the concept's and communication's strategy, the customer-experience design evolution, and the operational strategy, in order to support the investors and maximize their return on investment.

Sushi Bento—Kameari store

SKG CO., LTD. (Makoto Sukegawa), id inc. (Seiji Oguri, Yohei Oki)

Tokyo, Japan

118 square feet
(11 square meters)

2018

A new sushi bento brand by Wakahiro Inc., Sushi Bento is renowned for their rolled sushi and grilled mackerel sushi. With their passion to make sushi bento at a new standard, Wakahiro Inc. started this brand hoping that many people would be drawn to their high-quality sushi, going beyond ordinary bento.

Located in the busy location of Kameari in Tokyo, Japan, the store needed a fresh and effective interior. On the internal wall of the store, rhombus-shaped white tiles were placed on curled metal sheet. While conveying a simply look and finish to the interior at first glance, from a different viewpoint, it's reminiscent of rolled sushi. In addition, it complements the artwork, which is a motif of ingredients taken by photographer, Kazuhiro Kitahara.

Framed within a big wooden box-like structure, the design helps to gather and showcase the food selection, while providing a clean and well-organized impression. Inspired from Japanese traditional family

crests, Sushi Bento's logo contains hiragana "su" and "shi," kanji "ben," and also the shape of chopsticks and rolled sushi.

Villa de Patos

Savvy Studio
Saltillo, Mexico
2013

Villa de Patos is a family business, founded in 1980, that seeks to provide noble, natural, and healthy products. Their juices, cheeses, and Mexican sweets are produced by using traditional planting and free-range techniques, with special care towards the environment and the people inhabiting it.

For the Villa de Patos store in Saltillo, the idea was to replicate the brand's philosophy by using materials that express tradition, purity, and simplicity. Savvy Studio completed the branding and interior design for the Villa de Patos store, as well as the packaging design. Given that this store stocks more products than the other branches, a larger customer-care bar was needed—one that would be capable of displaying even more products—and also interior and exterior sitting areas.

The lighting design for the space was based on a very basic grid, leaving the fixtures exposed. Given the nature of the space, the furniture was designed to provide optimum flexibility, allowing for multiple

configurations within the store. Product displays play a principal role by displaying individual items for sale, each with their respective ID tags.

For the development of the brand, identity of the products, and other communication materials, the designers used handmade illustrations of products, vintage typography, and photographs from the owners in different times to convey the life cycle of this finely-crafted product, from origin to its commercialization.

CREPERÍA
PRODUCTOS del CAMPO
100% NATURALES
Solo una tierra sana produce alimentos sanos

C.P. 25950
VILLA de PATOS

VILLA de PATOS
Desde 1980

25950
VILLA de PATOS
Desde 1980

C.P. 25950
VILLA de PATOS

1
2
3

Cocada

Jugen

Anagrama

San Pedro Garza García, Mexico

700 square feet (65 square meters)

2014

Jugen is a wellbeing brand located in San Pedro Garza García that specializes in health foods, especially juices made from all-natural ingredients and super foods. As Jugen's products are created with the purpose of cleansing, healing, and detoxifying the body, the design proposal took inspiration from ancient herbal medicine bottles. To this, Anagrama added modules to communicate cleanliness, modernity, and order, much like in a modern laboratory.

For the interior design, Anagrama created a space that is a mix between a bar and an apothecary shop. The lighting, mostly natural light from the sun—together with the lush vegetation, the lab equipment and flasks, and the diverse books—created a natural, warm, and inclusive space. Simultaneously, Anagrama developed a graphic identity that transmitted health, wellbeing, and tastiness in a cheerful and friendly way.

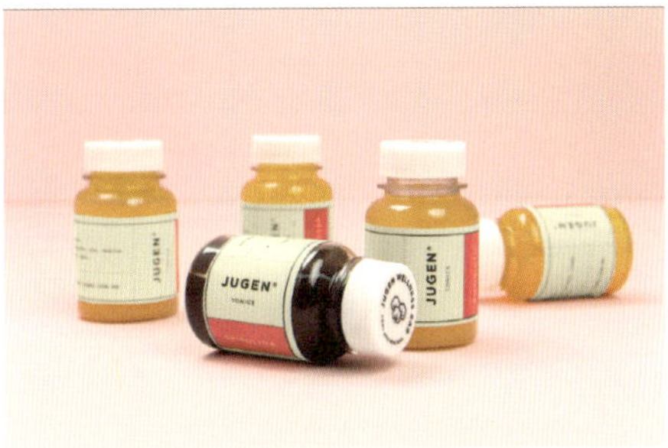
JUGEN®

JUGEN

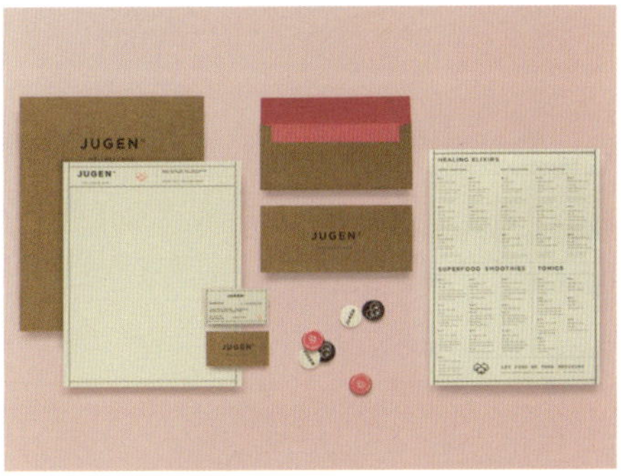
JUGEN®
HEALING ELIXIRS
SUPERFOOD SMOOTHIES
TONICS

JUGEN®

JUGEN®
WELLNESS BAR

Conversations: The Designers

Do you focus on interior design or graphic identity in your daily work? When you are responsible for both simultaneously in a project, what is the biggest challenge for you?

At id inc., we work as a team. In many cases, Oguri is in charge of the interior design and Oki is in charge of the graphic design. Depending on the projects, either of us takes a leading role. Cafe Ki is the first project we did for both interior and graphic design together. Since it was a project that put emphasis on the interior, the elements of interior design were reflected in the graphic design. First, we made a logo from the shape of furniture and developed original fonts from the logo. In order to convey in graphics what we meant in the interior, we repeated long discussions, shared the goal, and worked on the design. Since two different people design the interior and graphics, it was difficult to share the goal, but we think that the high level of expertise contributed to its quality after sharing it.

id inc.

An interview with co-founder of id inc.

Seiji Oguri

id inc. is a design office that was established in 2013 by designers Seiji Oguri and Yohei Oki. They are known to provide genuine design that evokes beliefs and emotions for a wide range of areas, including interior, product, and graphic.

What is the biggest difference between designing for a food brand to other product types? What makes a good food shop?

When dealing with food, we closely consider if the food provided there looks delicious. The impression can be controlled by extracting various factors from lighting to package design.

Are there any special requirements of design from the client of the brand? How do you satisfy your client?

The client of Cafe Ki had two contradictory requests—she wanted to be a space like an art gallery and also wanted the space to be full of plants. Pure white space does not make customers relax. On the other hand, if the place is full of plants, it requires a lot of care in a space that serves food. Extending the legs of the table and shaping it like a tree branch solved the contradiction. As a result, Cafe Ki has another function as a gallery and workshop space, displaying seasonal paintings and flower arrangement. It also inspires people's imagination with the branches of trees.

Is it difficult to balance interior design and graphic design in terms of time management? How do you allocate time and order?

As I previously mentioned, we work as a team. Because interior and graphics are often done by different designers, we manage time on our own. As designers we simplify whatever we can simplify and try to use more time for verification. So many discoveries are made through building a model, so we are conscious of producing the maximum effect in a limited time.

What are the key points to brand a food shop?

Obviously, it is important to make the food look delicious. In addition, we try to design the brand to be loved by customers.

How do you ensure connections between a shop's graphic design and interior design?

We value creating from a consistent viewpoint. Specifically, we try to match the color of the interior paint with the color of the graphic print and to keep the same impression in margins. On the other hand, we are mindful of not overriding the strengths of each other.

How do you ensure all design elements correspond to the core/idea of the brand?

Basically, we think about the idea to clearly express what the brand wants to convey. Needless to say, the message of the design and brand is consistent. There is no such thing as bringing designs from irrelevant places. We greatly value drawing out the beauty that the brand has.

In your opinion, what role does a designer/design team play when designing a food store? What do you want to bring to the brand through your design?

We believe that the designer's role should incorporate diverse perspectives. It is what the customer feels and the hidden beauty that should be made visible from the outside. What we want to express is to accurately convey the beauty of the brand to a broad audience.

What are your branding goals for the future?

I would like to make quantitative achievements in design. In order to make it happen, we think that it is important to collaborate with all experts such as photography, video, business, and marketing.

Is there anything you'd like to add about interior design and graphic identity of a food shop?

We think that the design of a food shop includes the moment they walk in to the space to the last moment that customers put the food in their mouths. For that reason, we believe that the interior of the food shop and graphics are equally as important. Also, it is important to realize what you can do to convey the beauty of the food shop.

Do you focus on interior design or graphic identity in your daily work? When you are responsible for both simultaneously in a project, what is the biggest challenge for you?

We typically develop projects as a team. The teams consist of interior designers as well as graphic designers. Therefore, both points of view are represented during the design process. The biggest challenge for the team is to develop the story behind the project. This forms the basis and core idea for the entire project. Once this is established, the team members can work more individually in different directions.

TOC. designstudio

An interview with co-founder of TOC. designstudio

Torsten Haardt

TOC. designstudio is a successful and lively office situated in Nuremberg, Germany. The name TOC stands for Transfer of Creativity. This is what it is about: Lateral thinking, a mix of disciplines, being wild and passionate, and keeping the best possible result for the client in mind.

What is the biggest difference between designing for a food brand to other product types? What makes a good food shop?

For us, there is no difference. Any project we develop needs to become something desirable and special. It needs to be loaded with emotions. There is no difference between a food brand to any other brand.

If there are special design requirements for the brand, how do you satisfy your client?

There are always special requirements from the clients, so we listen very carefully to understand the customers and their needs. It is actually an important part of the design process to keep those requirements in mind and still create a functional and aesthetic project.

Is it difficult to balance interior design and graphic design in terms of time management? How do you allocate time and order?

We develop interior and graphic design at the same time for the concept design. We believe this is very important as both departments need to come together. After this stage, the development of the two areas is more individual. The interior design will continue faster while the corporate design, web design, etc. takes more time.

What are the key points to brand a food shop?

For any project, it is important to get the foundations right. First of all, we need to develop the spirit of the project. From there, we can continue and tell the stories about enthusiasm, passion, and visions of our customers. Through mysterious or surprising settings, our projects thus become lasting beautiful experiences.

How do you ensure connections between a shop's graphic design and interior design?

The graphic and interior designers are in constant communication about the project. During the design process it will always be checked if the original idea and the spirit of the project is still seen. Only if all parties are happy with the result will it then be presented to the client.

How do you ensure all design elements correspond to the core/idea of the brand?

While working on a project, we have to keep the documentation of the core/idea visible in the studio. Our walls and pin boards are covered with the results of the initial design. It is important to keep it available as it is like a guideline that has to stay in focus at all times.

In your opinion, what role does a designer/design team play when designing a food store? What do you want to bring to the brand through your design?

We sometimes feel like the midwife delivering the brand for a food store. We help to develop the story and the visual design. We give it a face.

What are your branding goals for the future?

We feel responsible for the world that surrounds us and we would like to contribute to making it a little better every day. Our goal is to put this attitude in our projects and turn them into sustainable and fair projects.

Do you focus on interior design or graphic identity in your daily work? When you are responsible for both simultaneously in a project, what is the biggest challenge for you?

Mostly graphic design has the focus. An interior design project could take months. Therefore, in a year I finish much more graphic design works than interior design. It is a bigger challenge for me to create a unitary design, when one designer is responsible only for graphic design and another for interior design. I see the whole picture better when I can design everything.

kissmiklos

An interview with founder of kissmiklos

Miklós Kiss

Miklós Kiss's works incorporate various facets of architecture, fine art, design, and graphic design. A strong artistic approach and outstanding aesthetic quality characterize his art. His fine art pieces are just as significant as his distinctive style in corporate identity and graphic designs.

What is the biggest difference between designing for a food brand to other product types? What makes a good food shop?

There is no difference, I manage every project in the same way.

If there are special design requirements for the brand, how do you satisfy your client?

Before I start designing, I gather as much information as I can to pinpoint the problem I'm solving and determine the client's goals. I prefer it when the client trusts me completely and gives me a free hand.

I know clients want the best possible end result; so do I. Those who want to work with me will be sure that they get a strong concept with good design. But it rarely happens that clients don't know what they really want, or the owner of the project has been removed. In that case, I have to meet with the client and will try to talk about their concept again, asking a lot of questions to find the problem and the solution for their brand.

Is it difficult to balance interior design and graphic design in terms of time management? How do you allocate time and order?

I am very good at multitasking. Usually I have three or four different projects on in the same period. Every day, I work on several tasks, but I focus one at a time. Only when I have finished it do I start working on the next task. With this method, I can work on completely different projects in a day.

What are the key points to brand a food shop?

In my opinion, there always needs to be a strong connection between the product and the design. First, I always research the theme. Next, I try to figure out the concept before sitting down to design. It starts with a strong and solid concept—a strategy—that answers all the questions and sends the right messages to the customers.

How do you ensure connections between a shop's graphic design and interior design?

Concept and harmony are really important. In my work, everything is connected. You can find the same shapes, forms, colors, and feelings both in the interior and the identity design.

How do you ensure all design elements correspond to the core/idea of the brand?

Most of my clients wants to create a brand-new place or product, I rarely work with existing brands. It gives us huge freedom because we can figure out everything from the beginning. If I work for a brand that already exists, my task is to refresh their design. In that case, I go back to the roots and start the design process from the basics.

In your opinion, what role does a designer/design team play when designing a food store? What do you want to bring to the brand through your design?

Most designers have a recognizable style. Personal taste, style, and way of thinking means a lot when you design. For my part, I like to give a deeper meaning, a powerful visualization, and a memorable style to each brand.

What are your branding goals for the future?

I hope one of my works turns to a world-famous brand. In addition, I would like to create as many iconic places and brands as possible.

Is there anything you'd like to add about interior design and graphic identity of a food shop?

Less is more.

Union Atelier

Interview with executive director of Union Atelier

Minhan Lin

Union Atelier focuses on a combination of branding and interior design, making a comprehensive integration plan, and wedding European and American contemporary design trends and local culture with an international view of design thinking to create a unique design style. The oracle " 聿 " represents the action of holding a pen with a hand, which is also the first step in their creative thinking. The mission of Union Atelier is to achieve a well-cooperated platform between clients and designers, creating works that can meet clients' needs.

Do you focus on interior design or graphic identity in your daily work? When you are responsible for both simultaneously in a project, what is the biggest challenge for you?

We pay equal attention to branding and interior design. If the atmosphere of the space is not good, customers will not be impressed by the brand. Likewise, if the brand identity is not amazing, customers will not be drawn to the space. They are two sides of the same coin, so they should not be designed by different companies. When I was responsible for the interior design and branding of a project for the first time, the biggest challenge was how to combine these two themes completely, how to convert from two-dimensional vision to three-dimensional space, and then from three-dimensional to two-dimensional, while also thinking about what color fits the atmosphere that this space wants to present, and ensuring the color used on the brand's packaging was bright. At that time, I did a lot of research—from the client's usual way of communicating to selling to the types of products, target customer, price positioning, and even to what kind of music should be played at the store, all of which are included in my design plan.

What is the biggest difference between designing for a food brand to other product types? What makes a good food shop?

The most important thing for a food store is to make guests feel that the products it sells are clean and safe, so designers need to pay attention to the portability and practicality of packages while completing the graphic design, and to ensure that the color palette can make food appetizing.

If there are special design requirements for the brand, how do you satisfy your client?

I have designed many types of brands and our clients' requirements are always very important. The information and content that brands want to emphasize and convey to its customers are not the same, therefore, I need to carefully listen to the clients' needs and their brand stories, using design techniques to highlight the key points, solving problems that clients have presented as far as possible, and finding problems that customers have not thought of.

Is it difficult to balance interior design and graphic design in terms of time management? How do you allocate time and order?

It is difficult to take branding and interior design into consideration at the same time. Designers need to think comprehensively, making them fully integrated and highlighting their characteristics. In general, I will interview customers first to collect the core information and needs of the brand as far as possible. Then I will set the overall positioning of the brand from the brand name and logo and begin to conceive how to collocate the elements of interior design with the brand identity. It is hard and meticulous work. I feel very grateful that my design team integrates branding and interior design with me.

What are the key points to brand a food shop?

The key point of food store's branding is certainly to differentiate itself from other competing brands in the food-stores market, which is quite saturated all over the world. It's important to make food unique in the marketplace. Branding, packaging design, sign design, and menu layout are able to evoke customers' desires to purchase. There are quite a few old brands that have become the hottest brands or stores of the moment through design and planning, which is a pretty good example.

How do you ensure connections between a shop's graphic design and interior design?

Designers must review whether their design is complete from the beginning, thinking about whether branding is closely integrated with interior design and ensuring there is no improper place. They should set a time point for review at each stage and carry out these reviews with customers. To build a successful brand, any fixes and adjustments should be made before the design is finished.

How do you ensure all design elements correspond to the core/idea of the brand?

A very simple way is to look at whether elements are coordinated first. If one of them is dissonant with other elements, you must examine whether elements need to be adjusted. After details have been adjusted precisely, the outline of the brand will be drawn completely, and the direction and philosophy of the brand can be communicated to customers correctly.

In your opinion, what role does a designer/design team play when designing a food store? What do you want to bring to the brand through your design?

If we compare the brand to a dish, I think the designer plays the role of tableware—a brand is like a handmade dish. If there is no exquisite container to present it, it will not be finger lickin' good. People are sensory animals and dining is like a ritual. Beautiful tableware and a good dining atmosphere can make people focus on the food itself.

What are your branding goals for the future?

I certainly hope that shops that I design can be found worldwide and they can attract a large number of customers. I also hope to have my own design followers, so that more people can visit and have an even more in-depth understanding of the store brand because of the design.

Is there anything you'd like to add about interior design and graphic identity of a food shop?

Industries have their own exclusive market, but the food industry is a mass market. It is not difficult to create a brand, but to make the brand creative and unsubmerged, it is necessary to create a "brand in the brand" through repeated thoughts of design.

Credits

35 GRAMMI

Photography: Alessandro Zompanti
Client: 35 GRAMMI | cornetteria - caffetteria

Abarrotes Delirio

Photography: Savvy Studio

Belle Époque

Photography: Mind Design
Client: Belle Époque

BLANCHIER

Photography: PhotoBox (Atsushi Kamiya)
Client: Tsukasa Suzuki

Cadeau de Rincotté

Photography: PhotoBox (Atsushi Kamiya)
Client: Manabu Ninakawa

Cafe Ki

Photography: Norihito Yamauchi
Client: Cafe Ki

Casca

Photography: Lackó Szögi
Client: Róbert Ádok, Csaba Harmath, György Varga

Choya Ume Specialty Shop

Photography: Mikito Tanimoto
Client: Choya Umeshu Co., Ltd.

Ciambelleria Alonzi

Photography: P.E. Bellisario
Client: Ciambelleria Alonzi e figli snc

Citizen Sprout

Photography: Project M Plus (Meiwen See)
Client: Jennifer Jewett

Coconut Pastelería

Photography: Nihil Estudio
Client: Coconut Pastelería

Daniel Bakery

Photography: Marion Luttenberger, Michael Königshofer
Client: Hotels Daniel, Wiesler BetriebsgesmbH

DON JUAN coffee & cakes

Photography: Vladimir Paripovic

El Moro

Photography: Moritz Bernoully
Client: Francisco and Santiago Iriarte

Flour and Salt Bakery

Photography: Taiwan Land Development Group, Pentagram
Client: Flour and Salt Bakery

Gard'Ann Patisserie

Photography: Bálint Jaksa, Eszter Sarah
Client: Gard'Ann Patisserie

Gaudenti 1971—Vittorio Emanuele II

Photography: Pepefotografia
Client: La dolce passione s.r.l.

Home Bakery

Photography: Home Bakery
Client: Home Bakery

HI-LO Liquor

Photography: Bonnie Tsang
Client: Talmadge Lowe and Chris Harris

Jayde's Market

Photography: Project M Plus (Meiwen See)
Client: Thomas Plejer

Jugen

Photography: Caroga Foto
Client: Jugen

Julieta, Pan & Café

Photography: vitale
Client: Julieta, Pan & Café

Kinber Made

Photography: Kinber Made, Filter017, Straight Design
Client: Kinber Made

Kostarelos

Photography: Konstantinos Kontos
Client: Kostarelos Chr. Sons & Co I.P.

Laura's Bakery—Værnedamsvej

Photography: Johannes Torpe Studios
Client: Laura's Bakery

Lust auf Vollkorn—concept store

Photography: TOC. designstudio
Client: Pema Vollkorn-Spezialitäten, Heinrich Leupoldt KG

M Tang

Photography: Piao Yan
Client: M Tang

Maison Marou Saigon

Photography: Bite Studio (Wing Chan)
Client: Marou Faiseurs De Chocolat

Maruzen Tea Roastery

Photography: Mikito Tanimoto
Client: Maruzen Tea Co., Ltd

Maui Pops

Photography: Brandon Archibald
Client: USAI Investments

Meet Mia

Photography: Marita Bonačić
Client: Mia Salman

Mélimélo

Photography: Daniela Arcila
Client: Ana Karina Orellana

Milk Land

Photography: Yukihide Nakano
Client: Hokuren

Mister Baker

Photography: Mike Hook
Client: Mister Baker

Mökki

Photography: Gareth Gardner
Client: Ritz-Carlton Hotels and Resorts

Motín

Photography: Rodrigo Chapa

Pâtisserie Alex

Photography: Union Atelier
Client: Pâtisserie Alex

Pâtisserie Es-T

Photography: PhotoBox (Atsushi Kamiya)
Client: Masato Shiba

Pâtisserie Numorous

Photography: PhotoBox (Atsushi Kamiya)
Client: Yasuhiro Otsuka

PavoMea

Photography: Wang Yingfei, Yang Feng
Client: PavoMea Co., Ltd

Prossima Fermata—ice cream laboratory

Photography: Federico Villa
Client: PROSSIMA FERMATA - Laboratorio di gelateria

RL

Photography: Union Atelier
Client: Chun Rui Co., Ltd.

Sabah

Photography: Rodrigo Chapa
Client: Sabah

Softsrve Ice Cream & Dessert Bar

Photography: Wunderwall Design
Client: Softsrve

Spooning Cookie Dough Bar

Photography: Patrick Nitzsche
Client: Spooning Cookie Dough GmbH

Sushi Bento—Kameari store

Photography: shuntaro (bird and insect ltd.)
Client: Wakahiro Inc.

Tafelzier Patisserie

Photography: TOC. designstudio, Cristopher Civitillo
Client: El Paradiso Patisserie GmbH

Temper Chocolate & Pastry

Photography: Janis Nicolay
Client: Temper

Villa de Patos

Photography: Savvy Studio
Client: Villa de Patos

Winter Milk

Photography: Caroga Foto
Client: Winter Milk

Yí PATISSERIE

Photography: Onion, Kaho, Peanut
Client: Yí PATISSERIE

ZERO-e ice cream café

Photography: Alessandro Zompanti
Client: ZERO-e srl

Index

Nihil Estudio
P18
www.nihilestudio.com
nihil@nihilestudio.com

NINE associati
PP42, 156, 168
www.studionine.it
info@studionine.it

Out of Thin Air Studio
P34
www.yooobox.com
269359205@qq.com

Pentagram
P22
www.pentagram.com
newyork@pentagram.com

Project M Plus
PP120, 202, 208
www.projectmplus.com
info@projectmplus.com

Rice Creative
P152
www.rice-creative.com
rice@rice-creative.com

Savvy Studio
PP214, 224
www.vvstudio.net
hola@savvy-studio.net

SORABRAND
P90
www.sorabrand.com
sorabrand@sina.com

STIRIXIS Group
PP62, 218
www.stirixis.com
advance@stirixis.com

studio wok
P172
www.studiowok.com
info@studiowok.com

TOC. designstudio
PP30, 74
www.toc-designstudio.de
info@toc-designstudio.de

Union Atelier
PP98, 148
www.unionatelier.com
contact@unionatelier.com

vitale
P132
www.vitale.es
info@vitale.es

Vladimir Paripovic
P128
www.parchitects.wordpress.com
parchitects01@gmail.com

Wil Ken
P180
www.instagram.com/
wunderwalldesign
ken@wunderwalldesign.com

Zentralnorden
P192
www.zentralnorden.com
cs@zentralnorden.com

Published in Australia in 2019 by
The Images Publishing Group Pty Ltd
ABN 89 059 734 431

Offices

Melbourne
6 Bastow Place
Mulgrave, Victoria 3170
Australia
Tel: +61 3 9561 5544

New York
6 West 18th Street 4B
New York, NY 10011
United States
Tel: +1 212 645 1111

Shanghai
6F, Building C, 838 Guangji Road
Hongkou District, Shanghai 200434
China
Tel: +86 021 31260822

books@imagespublishing.com
www.imagespublishing.com

The Images Publishing Group Reference Number: 1532

NATIONAL LIBRARY OF AUSTRALIA

A catalogue record for this book is available from the National Library of Australia

Title: The Food Store: 50+ Stunning Interior Designs & Branding Concepts
Author: Paolo Emilio Bellisario [Introduction text]
ISBN: 9781864708424

Printed by Everbest Printing Investment Limited, in Hong Kong/China